ADMERGILL
with
BLACKO AND BROGDEN

THE HISTORY OF AN ANCIENT PENNINE ESTATE

JOHN A CLAYTON

Published By
Barrowford Press

2009

Cover design; Barrowford Press

www.barrowfordpress.co.uk
claytonj@talk21.com

ISBN 978-0-9553821-6-1

© John A Clayton

All rights reserved.

No part of this publication may be reproduced, stored in a retrieval system, or transmitted in any form by any means, electronic, mechanical, photocopying, or otherwise, without the prior written permission of the author or publisher.

Of standing stones and mound-cased bones,
Of dykes that scar the land,
Long ages past in landscapes cast,
By an ancient, knowing hand.

OTHER TITLES BY THE SAME AUTHOR

Valley of the Drawn Sword

An Early History of Burnley, Pendle and West Craven

ISBN 0-9553821-0-6
2006

The Lancashire Witch Conspiracy

A History of Pendle Forest and the
Lancashire Witch Trials

ISBN 978-0-9553821-2-3
2007

Cotton and Cold Blood

A True Story of Life, Love and Murder
in Victorian Lancashire

ISBN 978-0-9553821-6-1
2009

Pre-press by
Barrowford Press

Printed in the UK

BARROWFORD
PRESS

ADMERGILL
with
BLACKO AND BROGDEN

CONTENTS

ADMERGILL
with
BLACKO AND BROGDEN

THE HISTORY OF AN ANCIENT PENNINE ESTATE

John A Clayton
A.D. Hist. (Oxford)

Introduction

The modern OS maps show that the area of East Lancashire known as Admergill is centred upon a grid reference of SD 854 428. Covering some 840 acres of land within a distinct circle of man-made ditches it is fair to say that Admergill is an unusual place – even the very name is unique (as far as I am aware) within Britain. Within the following text it is intended to show that Admergill has preserved a number of important historical features within the landscape. Situated in a quiet valley on the very edge of Pendle Forest, astride the old Yorkshire and Lancashire county boundary, Admergill has been fortunate to escape the vagaries of the modern world and presents an unchanged face that would be recognisable to its early Medieval inhabitants.

Many secrets remain locked away within Admergill; the moorland heights show firm evidence of pre-historic settlement while the fields on the lower slopes hide a once bustling Medieval hamlet. An earthen mound, 100 feet in diameter and surrounded by a deep ditch, sits alongside the ancient trackway through Admergill and would once have controlled all through traffic within the area. Below the mound, by the side of the stream, we find a flat area known as the Mill Field where a now-lost watermill once stood. We shall also see that Admergill, although now a backwater hidden away from local industrial centres, was once considered of sufficient importance to have been the subject of dispute between kings, queens and nobility.

Furthermore, the valley through which the Admergill Water stream meanders forms an ideal funnel along which travellers have long made their way between Yorkshire and Lancashire. Indeed, before these two counties were ever conceived, Admergill would have seen a steady trafficking of stone, gold, bronze and iron goods as they were moved between the east and west coasts of northern England. The ridge-top 'highway' from Ribchester through to Kildwick would once have carried gold from Ireland, along with precious Lakeland stone implements, along the northern heights of Barrowford, through the Water Meetings to Admergill and along the flanks of Weets Hill to Barnoldswick.

The ultimate destination for these pre-Roman valuables was the Baltic where they were highly prized as trading goods. And so we see that within the mists of time anyone resident within the Admergill valley would have been ideally placed to control and benefit from a steady, lucrative national and international trade. This, of course, is long forgotten. The casual walker can be forgiven for passing along the footpath that shadows Admergill Water through the valley and seeing little other than the rise of the curlew or the burst of the bonnie-brown hare from his rest.

In the following we shall see that Admergill has much to offer the inquisitor if he or she knows how and where to look.

Chapter One

The Admergill estate is traversed on its eastern flank by the A682 Blacko to Gisburn road from which the observant traveller will notice that the moorland and rough grazing lands of Admergill sweep down from the heights of Burn Moor and Weets Hill to meet with the meandering stream of Admergill Water. This watercourse rises at Sandyford Head, on White Moor to the south-west of Weets Hill, from where it makes its way via the deep Sandyford Clough into Greystone Clough and turns sharply to the south-west. Having travelled for one kilometre from its source the stream now becomes Admergill Water, flanked for the rest of its journey by the steep sides of the 2.3 kilometre length of the Admergill valley.

Sandyford Head on White Moor

The infant Admergill Water rises at the point arrowed (SD861 444). The area gets its name from the large-scale quarrying of marl, or fine gravel, that was used to improve the land. People from Foulridge had common rights on the moor and the amount of marl removed from the Higher Sandyford area is apparent where the roadside embankments have been almost quarried away

Meanwhile, another stream is busy making its tumbling way down into the valley. Clauds Clough rises to the west on the heather-clad side of Burn Moor and for the whole of its 1.45 kilometre length forms the south-western boundary of the Admergill estate. Known as Oxegill in the Medieval period the clough meets with Admergill Water at a point known as The Hole (or Smithie Hole) where it then crosses Wheathead Lane (the ancient highway from Colne to Clitheroe). From this point the two streams become Blacko Water for 1.25 kilometres before emptying into the larger watercourse of Pendle Water at the Barrowford Water Meetings.

Clauds Clough forms the western boundary of the Admergill estate. It can be seen here on the left beneath the '1914 Bridge' at Wheathead Foot as it joins with Admergill Water (SD850 418).

The original stone clapper bridge over Clauds Clough is still in situ, now almost hidden by a modern wooden walkway.

This ford site was known as Wheathead Gate within Smithie Hole (or The Hole) and formed the crossing point of the ancient Colne to Clitheroe highway. The clapper bridge over Clauds Clough (Oxegill in the medieval period) served the trackway from Pendle Forest along the stream side to Admergill and beyond to Gisburn and Barnoldswick.

Admergill Water becomes Blacko Water as it leaves Smithie Hole through Bell Wood. The stream is then joined by Caster Clough before it meets with Pendle Water

Boundaries and their place within the landscape

In order to chart the evolution of a site, from a sparsely populated series of wet and hilly scrublands into the booming agricultural district of the Early Modern period, it is necessary to appreciate the importance of the land boundary as an entity beyond that of mere demarcation. The boundaries of our modern fields and meadows can tell us a great deal about the past, indeed there are times when the location and type of boundary are the only evidence that we might have for the existence of a long lost farm, field, settlement, principality or building. To this end the following text relates directly to the Admergill estate and is intended to provide at least an insight into features within our landscape that can so easily be overlooked but can, with a little consideration, tell us so much about our history.

The modern areas defined as *parishes* and *townships* are based upon a long and often troubled series of events. From the very first pre-historic settlers through to the post-sixteenth century period of the Early Modern the land holdings of our district have been in a constant state of flux. To a certain extent the extended area of East Lancashire, as distinct from its immediate neighbour of Yorkshire Craven to the east, was historically a backwater within northern kingdoms. As an easterly outpost of the Brigantes some 2,000 years ago we would have been subject to the authority of the Yorkshire-based tribal heads but the Ridge of Weets formed a barrier between the districts as indeed it does to this day. The upland moorlands of Weets Hill, Middop and White Moor have always separated the West Riding from East Lancashire and it can be no accident that the old county boundary was placed at this point.

It is fair to say that to the west of the old county boundary the Lancashire people have traditionally used Old English terms and phrases endemic within the Wessex-based kingdom of Saxon Mercia while our cousins over the Yorkshire border have their roots firmly within the Northumbrian tradition found within the Danelaw. There is, of course, nothing wrong with this; on the contrary these cultural differences provide our two districts with the character and tradition that endear them to the hearts of many. I use the Lancashire/Yorkshire boundary, and its powerful sense of division even in the nuclear age, as an illustration of the strength of boundaries within the psyche of the more warlike peoples within our colourful past.

The importance of boundaries throughout history cannot be overestimated; from the lord's manor and the worker's cottage to large and small settlements and countries - all required definitive boundaries that would be obvious within the landscape thus making the statement to outsiders *'this far and no further!'* Back in the mists of time land that would have been hard fought-for needed to be claimed and retained, new settlements needed to be firmly delineated.

Once a settlement had been occupied for a number of years its boundaries would have been obvious. As far as possible the limits were fixed along strong natural features such as rivers, streams, mounds, specific trees and escarpments within the landscape. Where none of these features were available to fix the new enclosures then it became necessary to create them through the digging of ditches and dykes, the erection of boundary mark stones and walls along with the planting of thorn hedgerows. It was then necessary to maintain these features; ditches had to be kept clear, hedgerows laid, stream courses managed and mark stones monitored for any signs of interference. It was vital that future generations of the community were aware of the history and extent of their settlement boundaries and this necessity gave rise to the ancient tradition known as '*beating the bounds*.' This is where the village elders would take the villagers, including the youngsters, on a tour of the settlement limits. The head-man would carry a gaily decorated staff and tap on the boundary mark stones with it; the magician's wand had its origins within the willow staff of the boundary beater and this latter would later evolve into the village Maypole.

The annual bounds outing was carried out on a certain day of each year and would ensure that the limits of the community-owned land were known to each following generation. Larger areas, such as the edges of the extended territory of a particular tribe, would have used natural features (as far as was practicable) for demarcation purposes; ridges, watersheds, rivers, valleys, cloughs, streams and rocky outcrops were all known as *'God's Boundaries'*. Ditches and dykes were sometimes edged with wooden palisades known as *'Pale-Dykes,'* these sites sometimes came to carry the name of *Palace*, an example of which can be found at Palace House in Burnley.

As later cultures took control of the ownership of land it passed increasingly into the hands of the individual as opposed to the community as a whole. Settlement boundaries were still perambulated in the *beating the bounds* tradition but land appropriation also needed to be fixed and this was done by a formal procession of local worthies around the land in question.

Where land had changed hands within the community local people of a high status would accompany the new landowner and vendor around the boundary in question and a narrative analogue would be used. This took the form of a spoken deed which became a form of property charter; henceforth an annual procession around the land established a right of tenure. The final words of the deed were '. . . *and by performing this service we hold our lands.*' Remnants of this formality could be seen even in the nineteenth century where written deeds contained the phrase '. . . *by a rod out of court was sworn*. . .' where the rod was a staff upon which a testament was sworn, hailing back to the origin of the staff used in the boundary procession.

Other cultures employed the tradition of encircling their land or property, the Egyptian Pharaohs walked around a fortified city as part of their coronation ceremony. Indian Rajputs would circumambulate a temple during its consecration; also Thai and African kings made the circuit of their palaces on their enthronement. Hittite and Malaysian rulers had to travel around their dominions in order to establish a right to them.

Roads are an important element within the system of ancient boundaries; they have a strong tendency to endure within the landscape and can be seen to be a strong anthropogenic feature, both in the indication of settlement, and in the continuity of land occupation. Boundary roads resemble other boundary features in as much as they provide an obvious linear limit but they differ in that they also provide movement into, through and out of that area.

Throughout our history five main boundary types were employed, these are **political, defensive, estate, parish** and **farm**; within these main categories were less important divisions such as field boundaries. The purpose of the latter was two-fold; firstly a ditch around the perimeter of a field would carry water and therefore act as useful drainage. Secondly the banking thrown up from the excavated soil was reinforced with stones and then a hedge (frequently thorn) was planted on the top, this provided a highly visible boundary that was also stock-proof.

Many of our ancient national tribal boundaries have been identified by the finds of Celtic coinage and also by the written evidence of Roman historians. The actual boundary ditch, or dyke, did not always form the definitive extent of a tribal kingdom; in areas of open plain and marsh there could be a zone of no-man's land up to twenty miles in width. Late Iron Age boundary zones were commonly used to make ritual deposits. These zones were usually river valleys or areas of wetland and have produced important concentrations of flint tools, metalwork and single coins; numerous finds of this type have been uncovered over the ages from the River Ribble.

Iron Age tribal boundaries survived into the Anglo-Saxon period and, in some cases, form the present county boundaries; most of our parish boundaries were established by the eleventh century AD when many tribal frontiers were incorporated into local administrative boundaries. The Romans kept many tribal boundaries to mark their *civitates,* these formed the main units of Roman local government. Following the collapse of Roman rule in the early fifth century AD many earlier Celtic territories in the north and west reasserted their independence, this ensured a strong continuity of boundaries from the Iron Age and early Medieval kingdoms.

Most ecclesiastical parishes were established during the tenth and eleventh centuries AD. Late Saxon ecclesiastical parishes very often follow boundaries of Roman and pre-Roman times but these are difficult to prove due to the lack of written evidence during the Medieval period. In some areas Roman villas have been found next to the parish church and manor house within settlements. Anglo-Saxon land and ecclesiastical charters detail estate boundaries from the seventh century, many hundreds were translated into English and show grants of land from the king to individuals or monastic establishments.

Saxon Medieval estate boundaries were marked by a *bivallate* or two-fold ditch; this was a hollow-way formed by a double ditch several feet in width and several feet below the modern surface with high banks. These ditches were very often back-filled at a later date and incorporated into the field, this means that a parish boundary may now run along the line of a single hedgerow. Very often this hedgerow will run across country for miles with other hedges running up to it, but never across it. Such hedgerows invariably comprise massive earthen banks which support a number of different tree species, the number of these within a given distance can be used in a formula to ascertain the age of a boundary.

An excellent example of a bivallate ditch can be found near Sandyford on White Moor.

The Greystone Cross probably marked the junction of the ditch and a trackway (SD 863 443)

The photograph on the previous page shows the 'double-ditch' at Sandyford, on the higher slopes of White Moor. This site can be reached by following the track from Gisburn Old Road, alongside Star Hall. The ditch would have formed the boundary of a Saxon estate and would come to separate the common lands of Colne and Foulridge (White Moor) from the lands of Barnoldswick in the later medieval period.

On the other side of the wall in the photograph (running left to right) is the ancient Admergill to Barnoldswick trackway that skirted the height of Weets Hill and eventually became what is now known as Folly Lane (*fole* = OE *people* ie., *public right of way*).

Saxon estates formed the basis of later ecclesiastical parishes and often shared a considerable length of common boundary with them, these were prominent natural, or man-made features. Where later parish boundaries appear to be out of context it is advisable to employ the use of a tithe map, rather than accept present day civil parish boundaries as these are often later political limits. Admergill is a case in point here, the civil parish boundary does not appear to fit the estate boundaries for reasons we shall see later.

Demesne farms (where the land was retained by the lord) on larger manors frequently included deer parks for the provision of sport and meat. Most of these were oval in shape but the local topography would dictate the final layout. The park would be around thirty to two-hundred acres in extent and contained woodland and pasture surrounded by an earthwork bank. The ditch was on the inside and would be topped by a palisade fence, wall or hedge with occasional 'leaps' to allow for the movement of deer. Most Medieval deer parks were broken up in the sixteenth and seventeenth centuries and incorporated into farms, the boundaries of which frequently include parts of the original park boundary.

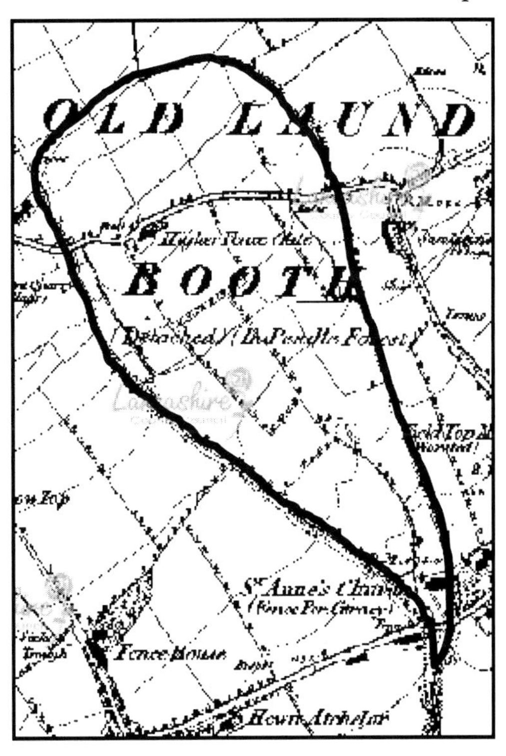

The map (right) shows a possible example of an oval enclosure or deer park in the Pendle Forest village of Fence.

The narrow end of the enclosure begins near to St. Anne's Church and runs up towards the ancient ridgeway track at Rigg of England Farm. This enclosure could be 'the fence' from which the village takes its name (SD 836 376).

Identifying Anglo-Saxon and early Norman farms can be done only where they were a single unit working a clearly defined block of land; within our East Lancashire area this type of agricultural unit was the norm as we did not have the open field systems around ancient nucleated villages that formed the estate centres of other districts.

Tithe maps relate to the taxes levied by the church upon each parish and are a valuable source of information on land ownership, field and farm sizes and the names of each field within the parish. Some areas are well served by tithe maps but Admergill is not particularly represented as a separate entity. The maps of our area available for study commonly date from around 1843 and show the parish and field boundaries as they existed at this time. Although some boundaries will have changed over time, Saxon and Norman boundaries can be traced with a little detective work. Where a boundary on the tithe map follows a man-made, or natural feature, such as a stream, hedge or lane, and they coincide with the parish boundary, then this would be the original farm boundary.

Boundary Markers

Of the various methods of boundary construction the most visible ones left to us are mark stones, ditches, banks, walled-banks, mounds and ancient hedgerows. Mark stones vary in size from pudding-stones measuring one foot in height to massive boulders weighing several tons. Care needs to be exercised in dating the standing stones that act as markers, many of these are Medieval boundary stones while a few will be monoliths dating from the Neolithic period. These latter examples are commonly found on the moorland heights and are often incorporated into the modern stone walls, or stand adjacent to the walls.

This example of a mark stone stands on the heights of Greenbank within Admergill and measures almost 1 metre in height and 1.5 metres across (SD 857 433).

Mark stones have been employed as boundary markers since time immemorial and the majority of them are now limited to areas of low level agricultural activity such as moorlands. Here they are most often placed at the junctions of public rights-of-way where footpaths cross trackways and boundaries. During the Puritan era of the seventeenth century a great number of the upright stone boundary and track markers were carved into the form of a cross; such an example existed on the Admergill/Blacko boundary at Blacko Bar but has been removed from its original position. Certain boundary marker crosses take the form of intricately carved stone 'wheel-crosses' and were often placed on parish boundaries. In East Lancashire these were relatively numerous as a pre-Norman workshop connected to the church at Whalley manufactured these crosses and they were erected throughout the parish of Whalley.

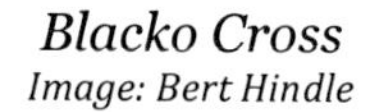

Blacko Cross
Image: Bert Hindle

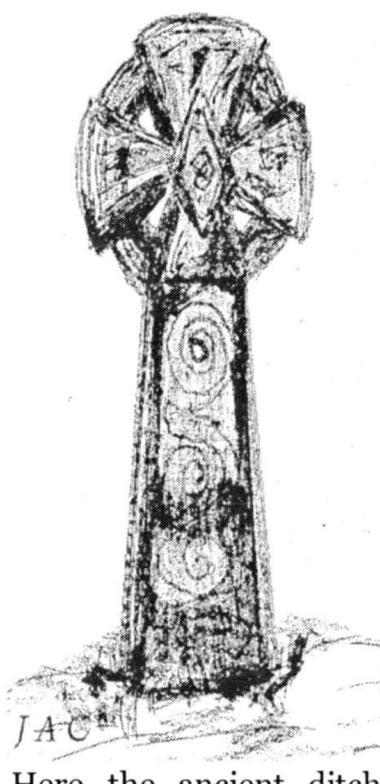

An example of a wheel-head cross.

The head of one similar to this was found at Alkincoats Hall and possibly once stood at Swinden where it marked the boundary between the townships of Colne and Great Marsden.

An unpublished Paper held by Nelson Local Studies Library (*Stone Crosses of Burnley and Pendle*) shows that a cross known as the Greystone Cross existed in the Admergill area. A study of a map dating to 1580 (of which we will see more later) shows that a cross is marked by use of the Hospitalier symbol †. With some effort we have been able to locate the (probable) point at which this cross stood and found it to have been placed where the ancient bivallate ditch shown in the photograph (page 13) at SD 863 443.

Here the ancient ditch meets the forgotten moorland trackway from Admergill to Barnoldswick (Folly Lane). If we are correct in the siting of the cross then it would have marked both the important former estate boundary between Greystone Moor (Admergill) and White Moor. It would also have stood as silent sentinel between the parishes of Whalley and the Cistercian parish of Barnoldswick.

It is impossible to distinguish the design of the Greystone Cross as no visible trace now remains (although it could have fallen and become buried) although there is a strong possibility that the cross was of the wheel-head variety - these were prized for their ornamental qualities and often removed while most plain upright crosses were incorporated into the early nineteenth century moorland enclosure walls. Alternatively, many ornamental crosses were destroyed by Puritans as they were offended by their extravagant ornamental symbolism.

The stone at the cross-roads has always been a rich source of myth for the folklorist; many tales are told of people selling their souls at a cross-roads or having experienced some supernatural event or other. The Celtic British were fond of burying executed criminals at cross-roads and this practice was echoed up until the eighteenth century when the same locations were used to erect the local gibbet in order to display the decomposing bodies of executed criminals. An example here is the Annel Cross which stood on the cross-roads below Pendle Hill by the old road known as Colne Gate (SD 816 426). Funerals heading for Colne, Newchurch or Downham passed this spot and the coffin bearers would rest the coffin on the stone and a prayer was said. The site of the Annel Cross (the word *Annel* suggests an early use of fire at this site, perhaps for ceremonial purposes) is shown on early OS maps.

The large boulders that slumber in the middle of fields, goading both tractor and plough, or the massive isolated stones seen only by the moorland venturer, are commonly dismissed as glacial erratics and given no more thought. Some of these large stones were indeed deposited by the glaciers that formed our landscape some 9,000 years ago but some have broken away from nearby rocky outcrops while others have been brought into the area for reasons known only to the people who placed them. Given the fact that man has walked among this scattering of stones since the retreat of the last ice-field it is likely that few of them remained untouched.

The Anglo-Saxons used the word *haran* in description of the many ancient stones they found within their newly settled English territories. *Haran* was gradually refined to *hoar* (as in the grey-white of a hoar frost) and shows that the stones carrying the appellation of *hoar* were already ancient when the Saxons arrived. The term *hoar* remained in relation to certain sites while others took on the English name of *grey* and we have a number of examples of these in the areas known as Grey Stones ie., at Dympenley in Roughlee and also on the outskirts of Barrowford where Pasture Lane crosses the ancient ridgeway and on the moor adjoining the north-western edge of Admergill. We also have an example of the earlier term *Hoarstones* in the village of Fence.

Rare surviving examples of boulder field enclosure walls are to be found along the ridge at Spen and Dympenley (SD 825 394). These are probably the stones that gave rise to the area becoming known as Greystones

Saxon *moots* were regular meetings of a community overseen by the local leader who heard the evidence put forward in land disputes and the like. The moots were held in the open air, usually at the site of some distinguishing landscape feature such as an ancient thorn tree or large stone. An Anglo-Saxon Gospel account for the Herefordshire area records:

Note of a Shire-Mote held at Aeglenoth's Stone in the reign of King Cnut, at which were present the Bishop Athelstan and Sheriff Bruning . . . and all the Thanes in Herefordshire.

Certain mark stones, then, were considered to be of great importance to communities, they had been placed for good reason and their position was sacrosanct. Even within the nineteenth century people were still been fined for moving or destroying boundary markers and the perpetrators of these actions could think themselves lucky that they had not lived in earlier times when the punishment for tampering with markers could be the death penalty. This is illustrated in '*Owen's Ancient Laws of Wales*' which states that:

. . . there are three other stones, for which an action of theft shall lie against such as shall remove them: maen tervyn (meer stone); maen gwyn gorsedd (white stone of session); maen gobaith (a guide stone); and his life shall be forfeited whoever shall do so.

Photograph courtesy of Jack Greenwood

These walls at Winewall formed enclosures within the vaccaries of the Forest of Trawden

The stones were split and book-matched but are unlikely to date from the same period as the boulder walls seen at Spen and Dympenley

Chapter Two

Admergill and the Map of White Moor

Boundaries were increasingly created and enforced as the settlement of incoming cultures progressed but the movement of people across these newly-settled lands was still necessary - trade routes, inter-tribal tracks and footpaths could not be closed. Medieval records make many references to *merc stones, marchstans* and *merestans*. The town of Nelson was formerly known as Great Marsden, the name Marsden grew out of the earlier *Merclesden (the valley of the monument)*. It is possible that the monument referred to in the naming of the district was the massive monolith standing on a man-made hill in the Shelfield area of Nelson on the lower slopes of Boulsworth Hill. This formerly monolith (SD 894 374) was vandalised in the Victorian period and transformed into what became known as Walton's Spire after the vicar who perpetrated its desecration.

It is interesting to note how close are the words *mark*, *merch* and *march* to the words *market, mercet* and *merchant*, especially as Medieval markets were centred around the market stone - these commonly had a later shaft added to become the market cross. There is also relevance in the fact that the god *Merc*-ury had the emblem of a standing stone. The variations of the word *mark* shown above all share the same root within the Old English word *mære* used to describe a boundary marker. In all probability, then, we see this within the name of Ad-*mer*-gill. *Gill* is a Scandinavian word which, in our particular area of East Lancashire, describes *a brook within a deep cutting/ravine*.

The *ad* pre-fix, however, is not so straightforward although it is possible to narrow it down to a small number of apposite meanings:

* We find that the Old English *æt* (pronounced *at*) means *near to* and this would translate *Ætmæregill* into *'near to the boundary gill.'*

* The Old English word *æd (ed)* is a pre-fix denoting a *turning* or *meander* (as in the turning of a watercourse). This would suggest an etymolgy within *Ædmæregill* of *'the turning boundary gill.'* This is exactly what Admergill Water does when it takes a double turn, each of ninety degrees, at Lower Admergill.

* The name of *Eadmer* was a common Anglo-Saxon given name; it was also the name of a Dark Age saint. The possibility that Admergill was held by a Saxon called Eadmer would give us the meaning of *'Eadmer's Gill'* and this is the most popular form of the etymology within *Admergill.*

Within modern etymology there are almost always disagreements as to exactly which root any given place-name might have had. Experts can narrow down the possibilities by use of a large number of precedents whereby a name has been proven to apply to a specific, such as a topographical feature. Because Admergill is such a unique name we do not have the luxury of expert **opinion** and it is, therefore, left to principals of 'best evidence' to get to the bottom of the matter. Within the following text we will be looking in detail at the many landscape features to be found within the Admergill estate and it is fair to say that somewhere among these will be the answer – we shall see!

For now it is fair to say that the name of Admergill appears to revolve around two reasonably safe etymological givens in *boundary* and *gill*. The suggestion here is that the gill formed the boundary and this has commonly been taken to be the watercourse of Admergill Water as it slides quietly through the valley. There is a problem with this, however; the Admergill valley appears to be far too broad in extent when it comes to the appellation of *gill* and, in support of this argument, a viable alternative is required.

Within our immediate area of northern England the terms *gill* and *clough* apply to a very similar landscape feature where the action of running water has formed a deep ravine. More often than not these ravines still contain a running stream or rivulet although broad dry ditches are often known as *clough*. It is interesting to note the subtle difference in the naming of each ravine-like feature by the early local settlers; the Saxons and Scandinavians had many names for what appear to us to be very similar hills, mounds, rivers, streams and hollows. Taking examples of the *gill* name around Admergill we see Blacko Gill, Caster Gill, Oxe Gill and Twirling Gill and it is fair to say that each of them closely resembles the other. There also numerous examples of *clough* in Admergill where we find Caster Clough, Greystone Clough, Clauds Clough, Wicken Clough, Dry Clough and Sandyford Clough. Some of these have carried both the names of *gill* and *clough* over the centuries and this lends weight to the argument that they applied to almost identical features.

A typical clough or gill feature within Admergill

In other northern areas, notably the Danelaw districts of Yorkshire and the Lakes, the term Ghyll can be found to apply to a small valley, or a wide chasm between rock outcrops. This is rarely the case in East Lancashire and the sheer size of the Admergill valley would seem to preclude it from having been the *gill* in Admer-*gill*. If the Admergill valley was not the gill, then, where was it?

This is where an invaluable historical record known as the *Map of White Moor* comes into play. Born out of a land dispute between the tenants of Foulridge and Barnoldswick in 1580-81 this map was created as a survey of the landholdings within the vicinity of White Moor, in the parish of Barnoldswick, to be presented to a land tribunal.

The map was originally unearthed within the bowels of the London archives many years ago by the noted Colne historian, Wilfred Spencer. Realising the importance of such an accurate and early document of local lands Wilfred brought a copy of the map home and placed it in Colne Library. Here, in 1977, the map came to the attention of another noted local historian, Stanley Graham of Barnoldswick, who set about converting its somewhat obscure notations into a clear version. Stanley wrote a Paper on the subject of the map and this is deposited at Barnoldswick Library. It is thanks to Stanley that I first became aware of the map and it so fascinated me that I have pored over it for years in an attempt to place the 1580 landscape within that of the modern day. This study has shown that the map is based on a scale of six inches to one mile and is surprisingly accurate. This has allowed for the location of lost and abandoned boundaries and this knowledge, coupled with early estate records, provides for a view of the landscape that has been lost to us for centuries.

The map is particularly useful in relation to the subject of this Book showing as it does the entire system of ancient boundaries around Admergill in relation to the wider aspect of the Yorkshire land holdings of Barnoldswick and Middop. This has allowed for the precise location of a lost hamlet within Admergill, the details of which will be seen presently.

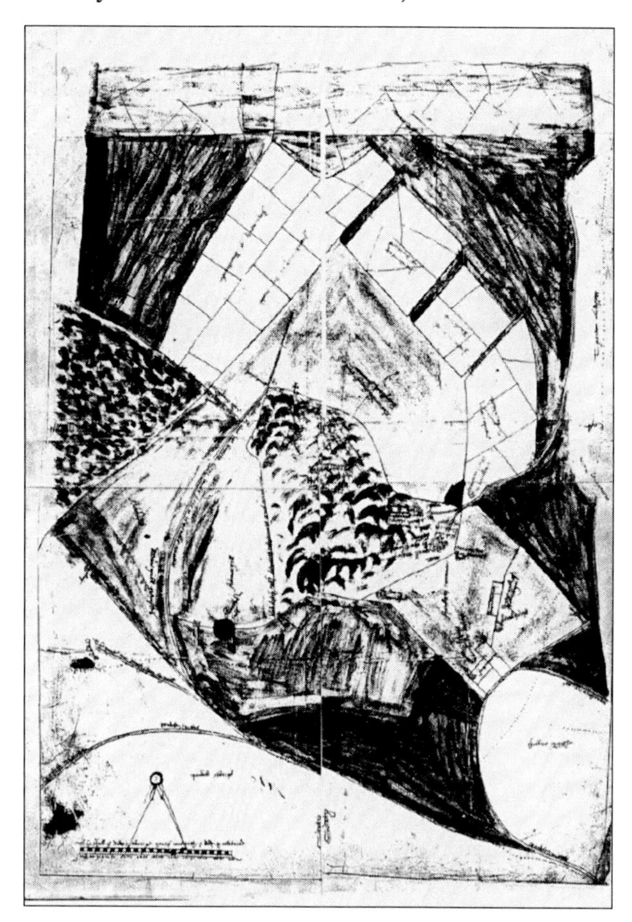

The original White Moor Map
Image courtesy of Stanley Graham

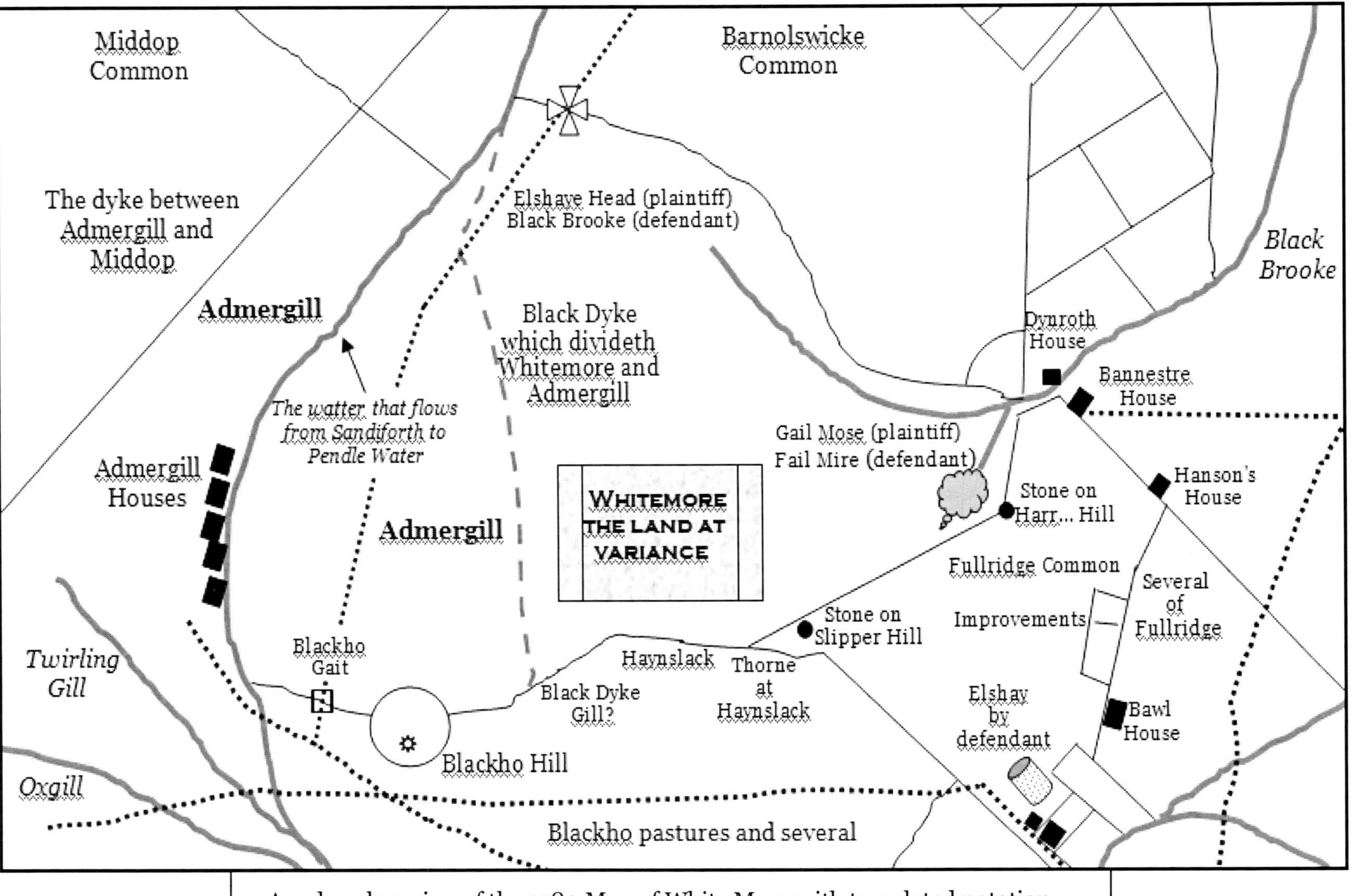

A reduced version of the 1580 Map of White Moor with translated notation

Note by Stanley Graham on the White Moor Map:

> *The original of this map is held in the Public Record office in London. Catalogue reference: Page 507. 3437 Barnoldswick 1580/81. (DL 31/106). There is a copy in both Colne and Barnoldswick libraries.*
>
> *The DL31 class is an original collection of maps from the Office of the Duchy of Lancaster. It is not certain which record this map relates to but there is a contemporary endorsement which implies that a lawsuit was involved. There is a much later endorsement which suggests it was drawn as evidence in a suit between the Tenants of Foulridge and the Tenants of Barnoldswick.*
>
> *In the Calendar of the Duchy Chamber Proceedings there is mention of a suit in 1580/81: Tempest et al. Tenants of Barnoldswick versus Bannester et al. Tenants of Foulridge. [DL31/123 T.1]*

Ditches and Dykes

As a rule the ditch and the dyke are differentiated from the clough and the gill by the fact that they are man-made. Not all ditches and dykes are old and by no means all of these will form any kind of boundary. Many field ditches were created to carry drainage water from land drains when waste land was upgraded to agriculture. Likewise, many dykes were created as land drains but they were often intended to carry a higher volume of water than ditches. The size of the dyke is generally much larger than the ditch and it is fair to say that the long, wide examples, such as Offa's Dyke between England and Wales, were intended as nothing other than a means of controlling the movement of people.

Within areas of intense agricultural activity many ancient ditches and dykes have disappeared beneath the plough but we are fortunate within our Pennine district as the uplands of the Pendle and Bowland forests retain their integrity within the landscape. No better proof of this latter statement can be found than the example of the Black Dyke. This dyke is an impressive earthwork of such dimensions as to render it of importance to the history of the whole district.

The Black Dyke runs over the top of the ridge between Admergill and White Moor and for most of its 1.3 mile length follows an almost straight north/south course. Technically this means that the feature can be considered to be of the type known as a *'cross-dyke.'* It is possible that the dyke is much longer than its straight ridge-top length as it takes a ninety-degree westward turn at a point known as the Black Dyke Nook (*nook* = corner) from where a continuous ditch runs over the ridge of Blacko Hill and down into Wheathead Foot. However, this latter ditch is described in a sixteenth century document and does not appear to have been considered to be part of the main dyke. It is safe, then, to consider only the length of ditch separating Admergill from White Moor as the true Black Dyke.

The northern end of the Black Dyke below Star Hall (SD 862 439) looking over the wall from the land known as The Longroyde (on White Moor) to Judde Field (Admergill)

At its northern extent the dyke is shown on the 1580 map as deviating from a line below Star Hall and running up to join the infant Admergill stream at Sandyford. Here the dyke crossed the stream at the point where Sandyford Farm now stands and this was the original 'Sandy Ford.' The ford is now located on Gisburn Old Road below Star Hall but this is not the original site. From Sandyford the dyke turns west and crosses the Gisburn Old Road before heading up the hill. It then dives down Greystone Moor and along to the Level of Weets Hill before rejoining the Gisburn Old Road (here no more than a hollow moorland track known as Coal Pit Lane) to pass the Ridge of Weets, Newfield Edge and down to the old road at Lane Side.

Carrying straight on at Laneside the ancient hollow road continues with its heavily tree-lined banks down to Coverdale where it meets with the equally ancient Howgill Lane. A couple of hundred yards along the way it passes a point where the Roman road from Brogden Lane on its route to Rimington crosses (SD 844 468). Carrying along its route the way passes the ancient earthwork at Bomber, then on to Whin Hill and beyond to Gisburn. For most of its length over the moor this route formed the Middop/Coverdale boundary and is marked by a number of boundary stones.

During the passage of time the bottom of the Black Dyke has filled in to a certain extent. Having said that, it is still possible to gauge the original size of the dyke and it is clear that someone, at some time, thought it necessary to invest a great deal of manpower in the building of this feature.

Ditch and dyke boundaries are difficult to date without firm archaeological evidence and we can only refer to available written evidence in order to fix a latest date for these features. Theoretically, then, we would need to rely on the records showing land transactions and disputes within the area (such as the Clitheroe Court Rolls) and unfortunately these provide little evidence other than the type shown below;

- ***1540:*** *John Hartley and Bernard Hartley complain against Robert Blakey in a plea of trespass for open fences between Juddefield and the Long Rodes upon a dyke called 'Le Blacke Dyke'. Jury award damages.*

- ***1583****: Interrogatorie; James Robinson aged 80 states that in 1523 the tenants of Barrowford exchanged lands with tenants of Blacko. Lawrence Hartley of Barrowford exchanged with James Hartley of Blacko and that Blacko in Barrowford joins another parcel called Blacko in Admergill and that a ditch divides the said grounds.*

LEFT: The Black Dyke Nook above Blacko Hillside Farm (SD 864 424)

RIGHT: The boundary ditch over Blacko Hill from Black Dyke Nook

The farm estate records of Ightenhill Manor state that in 1296 *'the heye about Blakey was made'* and this refers to the setting of the Blacko boundaries. There is little doubt that the boundary system referred to was that dividing Barrowford, Roughlee, the southern part of White Moor and Foulridge but this did not include the Black Dyke. Fortunately we have another record to consult and this compliments the 1580 White Moor Map perfectly.

Soon after the Norman Conquest the powerful de Lacy family became the overlords of a great deal of land, especially in the north of England. In the year 1147 Henry de Lacy granted the township of Barnoldswick to Abbott Alexander, of Fountains Abbey, in order for him to establish a monastic settlement there. At this time land transactions on this scale were executed by means of official charter whereby the land owner swore that he had perambulated the land in question, along with witnesses, and the land within the boundaries of that perambulation were to pass to the grantee. To prove the charter of his grant to Fountains Abbey de Lacy recorded the boundaries in some detail. He noted that Admergill was part of Barnoldswick and proceeded around the estate so as to ensure that it was included within his grant.

In his '*History of Barnoldswick*' Warner quotes the 1147 charter in relation to de Lacy's perambulation of Admergill:

> *By the stream called Blakebroc up the moor to Gailmers and so directly to Ellesagh across Blacko hill to Oxegill and up Oxegill to the Pikedlawe called Alainset thence to the ancient ditch between Middop and Coverdale.*

Here, then, we have a first-hand account of the twelfth century boundaries. Although none of the names in the charter survive it is possible, by use of field and map work, to accurately locate their positions. The *Blakebroc* is the *Black Brook* which flowed from White Moor into what is now the White Moor reservoir. This large canal reservoir was built in the early nineteenth century and there was good reason for the engineers choosing that particular site. There already existed a body of water there where the water from White Moor collected in a depression. On the 1580 map we see that this water was called *Gail Mose* and *Fail Mire*, depending upon whether you asked a Barlicker or Foulrigger, and this is the *Gailmers* of the charter.

From here the Black Brook flowed down the hill as what is now known as County Brook where it powered the water mill of what is shown on the map as Dynroth House in the Black Brook (this became Midge Hole Mill). Here, then, on the Foulridge boundary, Henry de Lacy and his men mounted their horses and proceeded to ride up the brook to Gailmers.

The drained White Moor reservoir with the site of Gailmers still holding water. (SD 878 437)

Photograph courtesy of Stanley Graham

This would not have been a strictly accurate description of de Lacy's perambulation as the Foulridge boundary at this point ran parallel to the modern Barnoldswick road. The original line can still be followed across the fields at the top of County Brook Lane where it was marked by a massive marker stone. This boulder can still be seen just to the west of Lark Hill Farm where it forms part of the roadside wall (inset right) and is marked on the map as the Standing Stone on Harrock Hill. *Hār* is the Old English for *grey* and the probability is that the name of the hill is actually Harrac Hill (*Old Oak Hill)* from *Hār-ac*. The marker stone here was immediately adjacent to Gailmers and the water would have been a more distinguished mark point with which to illustrate the charter.

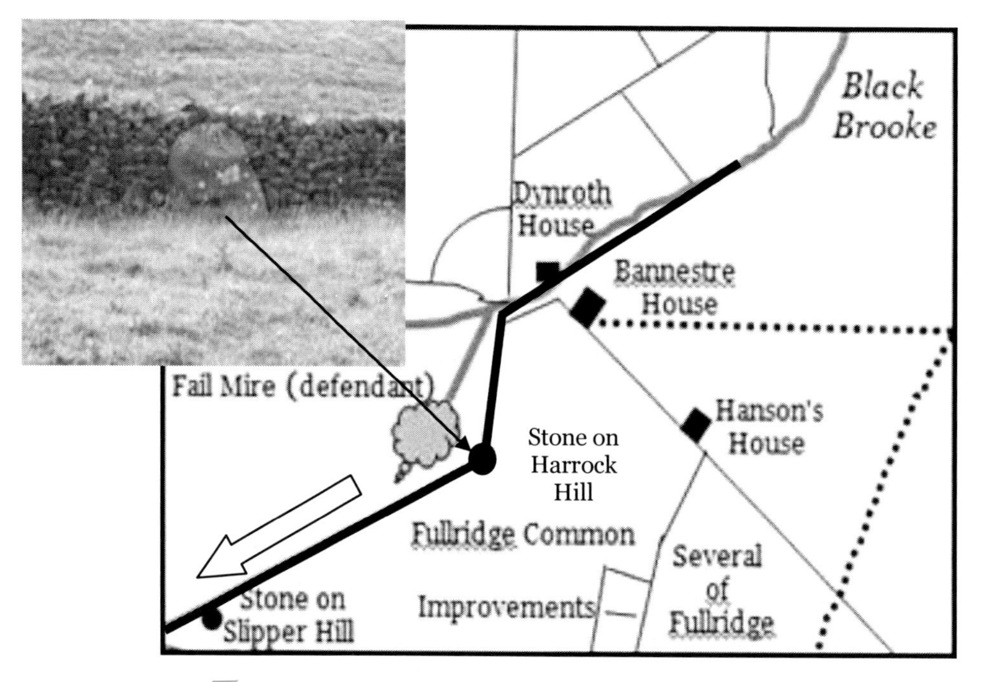

The first leg of de Lacy's perambulation took him up the Black Brook to Gailmers (Gail Mose/Fail Mire) and directly to Ellesagh

From Gailmers, or Harrock Hill, de Lacy then proceeded directly to Ellesagh. Whitaker, in his '*History of Whalley*,' has it slightly different in as much as de Lacy went; . . . *et ita in directum usque ad caput de Gleslagh*. . . which my pigeon Latin translates as; *and thus straight to the head of Gleslagh*. The temptation here is to assume that de Lacy made his way up White Moor to what is marked on the map as *Elshaye Head*. There is a problem here, however, as the perambulation follows from Elshaye over Blacko Hill and this would mean de Lacy making his way the mile down White Moor without mention of the boundary that he followed. If this were the case he would either have retraced his movement along the Black Brook up White Moor, which cannot be right, or he followed the Black Dyke back down to Blacko Hillside where he picked up the ditch over the hill. This is also unlikely as he does not mention the major boundary feature of the Black Dyke as he surely would have done. Furthermore, perambulating the boundary from Gailmers up to Elshaye Head, and back down to Blacko Hill, would have separated Admergill from Barnoldswick, the very thing that de Lacy did not intend to do.

It is almost certain, therefore, that the *Ellesagh* in Warner's account, and the *Gleslagh* in Whitaker, are one and the same name for the landscape feature above Malkin Tower known as *Haynslack*. This meant that de Lacy followed straight from the marker stone on Harrock Hill to the *Stone on Slipper Hill* which stood by the original track from the junction of Gisburn Old Road and Barnoldswick Road to Pasture Head Farm. Passing the stone, which marked the old Foulridge/Blacko boundary, de Lacy came to the *Thorn at Haynslack*. This was another prominent boundary marker and stood at the north-western corner of the garden at Pasture Head Farm. This thorn tree is mentioned as a boundary marker in the Clitheroe Court Rolls where, in the sixteenth century, it was said to have been *'the thorne near to John Hartley's house.'* At this point the modern White Moor/Blacko boundary is marked by Blacko Gill as it flows down from the Black Dyke Nook. This, however, was not the case in 1580 as the boundary on the map follows a forgotten ditch (possibly a trackway) higher up than the Blacko Gill from where it climbs the moor before diving back down to meet the Black Dyke Nook.

From here de Lacy travelled over *'the Blacou Mountain'* to *Oxegill*. This part of the boundary is extant in the form of a ditch along the ridge of Blacko Hill, now clearly visible as the modern enclosure wall runs along it. The ditch can be seen at Blacko Bar where the A682 interrupts its journey down Wheathead Lane into the bottom where it meets with Clauds Clough (*Oxegill*). This part of the boundary, over Blacko Hill and down into Wheathead Foot, is where the boundary known to Henry de Lacy differs from that in existence at the time that the 1580 map was drawn – the reason for this we shall see presently.

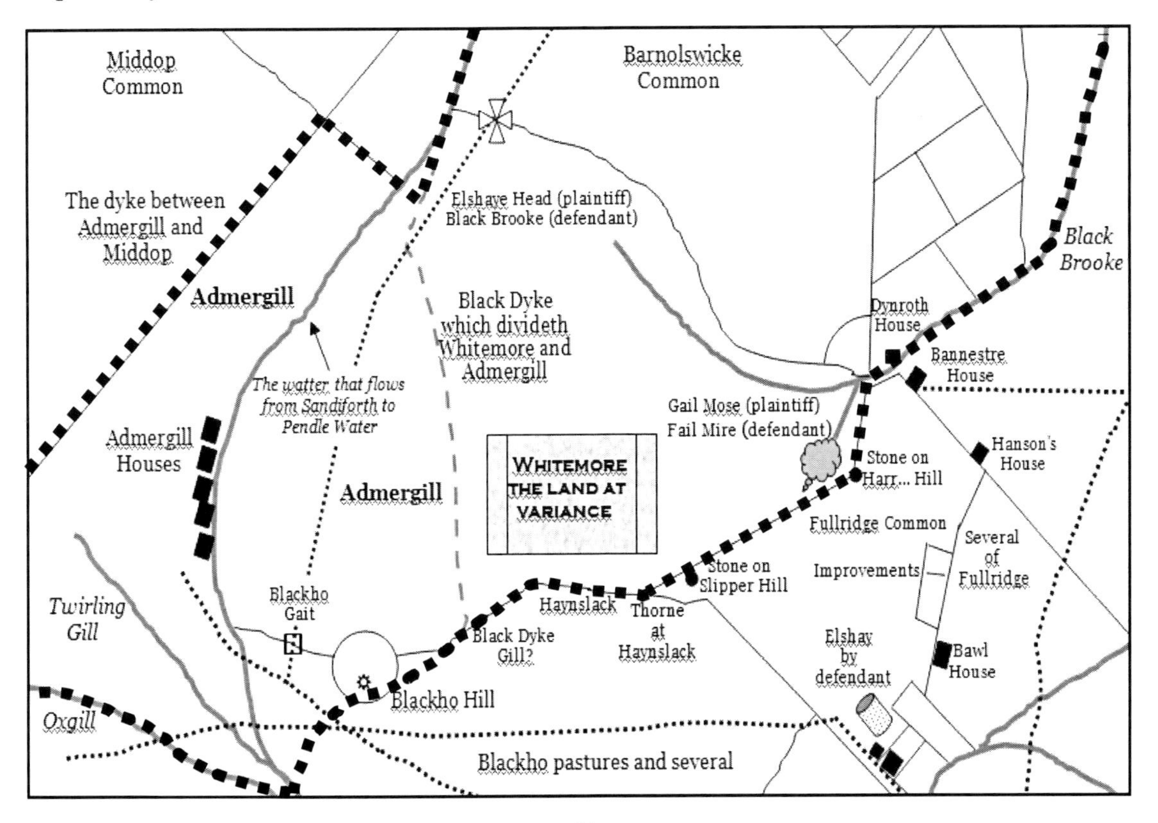

De Lacy's perambulation is shown on the previous page. It is noticeable that the boundary on the White Moor map does not correspond exactly with the perambulation from Blacko Hill to Admergill Water. It does not pass directly over the centre of Blacko Hill, as does the de Lacy boundary (and the modern boundary) because the 1580 map shows the hill before the northern half of it was completely quarried away. The hill on the Admergill side was far larger than the one we now see. To illustrate this, the position of Blacko Tower is shown – the tower now stands in the centre of the hill.

De Lacy continued his tour of the Admergill boundary by heading up Burn Moor along Claudes Clough (*Claud* probably derives from the cloud berries that grow in moorland situations – the first OS maps noted the clough as *Clouds Clough).* The clough rises higher up the moor and at this point a gulley known as Jackson Slack (*slack* = OE *hillside hollow*) takes over the stewardship of the Admergill boundary for a short distance. The boundary then meets a long moorland ditch at right-angles and this is shown on the 1580 map as *The dyke between Admergill and Middop* - this is the northern limit of the Admergill estate.

Near to the junction of Jackson Slack and the northern dyke stands a hill known today as Jackson Hill after a family by that name who farmed the nearby Jackson's House Farm in the nineteenth century. This hill is not marked on the 1580 map, probably because it actually stands on the Middop side of the Admergill boundary and was unnecessary for the purposes of the map. However, we see that the de Lacy charter shows Henry rattling *up Oxegill to the Pikedlawe called Alainset* and here we see that *Alainseat* is the old name for Jackson Hill. This was the summit of Burn moor (1,250 feet) and was an important point on the boundary of the Percy fee in Craven. Warner states that it; . . . *owed its name doubtless to a perambulation personally conducted by Alan de Percy in the time of Henry I.*

The description of *pikelaw* refers to the shape of the hill as the Old English *pike* means *pointed* and *lawe* is *hill.* The meaning of *Alainseat* may not be as Warner suggests, however, as *saeta* is the Old English description of a *land holding* or an *estate holding* while *seht* means *settlement. Ælan* means *to burn, set on fire* and this would provide a meaning for the name *ælanseht* of '*the settlement beacon.*' This is interesting as many other pikelaw hills are known to have been beacon hills.

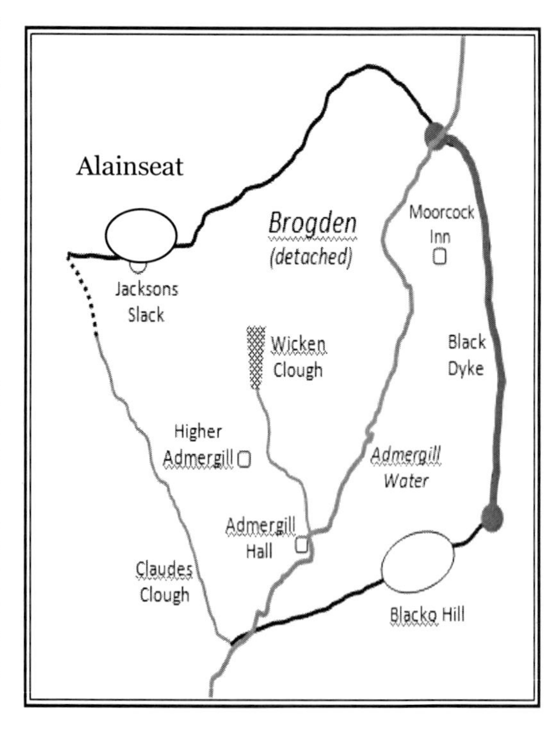

This brings us back to the subject of the origin of the name *Admergill.* Having already seen that the prefix *ad* has more than one possible root we can throw another spanner into the works – *ād* is the Saxon word for *mound of fire or flame, funeral pyre* and here we see a definite correlation with the fire-related appellation of *ælan. Ælanseht,* then, could be *the settlement beacon* or *ād (fire mound) in Ad*-mergill. This gives us the apposite meaning of *'the gill by the boundary beacon.'*

Here, then, we find an argument for Admergill being closely related to the pikelaw of Alainseat and, if this was indeed a beacon mound, this further suggests that the area formed an integral part of a wider community. Individual beacons were commonly part of a warning system whereby settlements could communicate with each other over long distances, especially in times of danger, such as the threat of invasion. There is also a consideration with regard to the fire aspect of the pikelaw that it could have been a ritual site for religious ceremonies or cremation. These hilltop mounds are commonly pre-historic tumuli, or burial barrows that have been adapted by each following culture to their own needs. The fact that Alainseat carries an Old English name strongly suggests that any use of fire on the mound would have been related to the Saxon, or Scandinavian use of beacons.

Looking NW across Green Bank as it climbs out of the Admergill valley. The summit of Alainseat is arrowed (SD 844 435). From the Lancashire side the pikelaw does not stand out to any degree but is very prominent from the Yorkshire side of the ridge upon which it stands

The northern extent of Admergill having been reached, de Lacy progressed eastward along the ridge-top ditch dividing Admergill from Middop . . . *thence to the ancient ditch between Middop and Coverdale.* This means that he traversed to the south of Craven Laithe Farm and onto Greystone Moor where the boundary ditch met with the ditch that runs from the end of the Black Dyke at Sandyford Clough northward across the Greystone Moor and down to Gisburn via Howgill and Coverdale as described earlier. This, then, was the extent of the Admergill limits.

Chapter Three

The Unsettled Boundary

So, Henry de Lacy considered Admergill to have been part of the township of Barnoldswick and in 1147 he generously donated the whole shooting match to the Abbot of Fountains Abbey. The reason for this is that Henry had fallen seriously ill shortly before his grant and he swore that should God allow his recovery he would show his gratitude in the best way he could think of. And he was true to his word.

However, there was a fly in the ointment in the shape of the true owner of the land. Hugh Bigod, Earl of Norfolk, heard of Henry's generous donation and was not best pleased. It turned out that Bigod was the true owner in that he held the Barnoldswick area directly from the king; the de Lacy family were, in fact, undertenants of the land and were not empowered to sell, or indeed give it away. Moreover, for many years the de Lacys had neglected to pay the annual rent of five marks and one hawk for their Barnoldswick landholdings. The fact that they had been able to get away with this no doubt meant that Henry de Lacy considered the estate to be his by default. He soon knew differently when the Abbey at Fountains were required to return the lands to Hugh Bigod.

Being a trifle upset at this Abbott Alexander approached the king (Henry II) with a plaint of dispossetion. The king was sympathetic to the abbot's plea and duly summoned Bigod to his court where he pointed out that Bigod was mortal and therefore required the intercessions of the Holy Church for the safety of his soul. Even more persuasive was the king's argument that the crown actually owned the land and, taking the king's point (probably because he had little other choice) Bigod hastily restored the lands to the abbey

Now, things bumped along for a couple of centuries but during that time there was never any legal definition of the boundaries around Admergill nor, indeed, was the boundary between Lancashire and Yorkshire settled. In 1287 the Earl of Lincoln, a descendant of the Henry de Lacy who perambulated Admergill in 1147, lent the sum of 350 marks to the Abbey of Kirkstall. The original Fountains Abbey settlement in Barnoldswick had failed and the monks subsequently moved to Leeds where they set up the new Kirkstall foundation.

By 1287 the abbey here found itself indebted to Jewish money-lenders who were pressing them hard for repayment and this is where the Earl of Lincoln stepped in. The monks gratefully accepted the money and duly paid their dues but there was to be a sting in the tail. The earl had been given *'certain lands within Blakeburnshire'* as security for his money and, the Lancashire border of Blackburnshire being notoriously unsettled, he considered that Admergill formed a part of his Lancashire grant. This being the case, about the year 1300, the earl took for himself the 840 acres of Admergill that lay within the Barnoldswick landholdings of Hugh de Grymston, Abbott of Kirkstall. This land also included the area marked on the map of 1580 as *'Whitemore the land at variance'* and so we see that, despite the charter of Henry de Lacy in 1147, this western limit of Barnoldswick had been in dispute for over 400 years by the time that the White Moor Map was drawn up. Here, then, we have the probable reason for the 1580 dispute in that the tenants of the village of Foulridge considered that the White Moor was theirs by right of common and had been since at least 1300 when the Earl of Lincoln had returned it to the Lancashire parish of Colne (within which Foulridge fell).

Our subject area, then, was in continual dispute to the extent that abbotts, nobles and kings were amassing records relating to its ownership by the cartload. And now it was time for a queen to join in. To muddy the historical waters the de Lacy lord of Clitheroe surrendered his large Yorkshire landholdings at Pontefract to the king in 1292 and this meant that Barnoldswick was held by Kirkstall Abbey directly of the Crown. In the early fourteenth century Edward III made a grant of the Forest of Blackburnshire to his mother, the dowager Queen Isabella, and from various sources we learn that Isabella was no pushover when it came to retaining her lands and so it proved with the disputed Barnoldswick estate.

The Queen's Lancashire foresters constantly entered the manor of Barnoldswick and her chief forester, Richard de Merclesden, demanded *puture* from the Barnoldswick tenants. This meant that the Queen's men could demand food and drink for themselves, their horses and dogs on a certain day each week. Naturally the abbott (at this time one Hugh de Grymstone) was miffed at this and the Close Rolls of 1335 show that he had complained directly to the king who ordered an inquiry at Nottingham under the auspices of Justice Geoffrey le Scroop. The abbott complained of the long delays in the matter whereby writs, orders and inquiries over many years had still not concluded the affair.

There were two apparent reasons for the Crown's indecisiveness. Firstly, it was reluctant to give up a part of what was considered to be hunting forest as these areas were jealously guarded at that time. Secondly, it was unclear as to exactly where the Lancashire/Yorkshire border lay. The king, therefore, ordered a jury from each county to be empanelled to try the case, no doubt with further interminable wrangling. The land itself was of small value, for it is stated to be *'sour' (morosa)*, worth only a *'halfpenny an acre'* and consisting of *'rough uncultivated pasture fit only for large animals to feed upon.'* It was the hunting over it which made it valuable.

Another Close Roll holds a document addressed to John Giffard who was the king's escheator north of the River Trent, in other words the man responsible for overseeing the forest lands in northern England. The document quotes Henry de Lacy's original foundation to the abbey of Fountains and Henry II's re-granting of Barnoldswick to Kirkstall. There then follows a description of Queen Isabella's foresters who trespassed on the Barnoldswick lands which were outside of her (Pendle Forest) lands of Blackburnshire.

The text goes on to state that the Kirkstall Abbey had the sympathy of the Blackburnshire steward but he was not willing to intervene in the matter as he understood that puture had been charged against the tenants of Barnoldswick for generations and he would, therefore, require direct guidance from the king, or Queen Isabella, on the matter. The king had ordered that the Queen's men desist from exacting puture from Barnoldswick but with the caveat that Kirkstall should pay compensation in the form of a 'fine' amounting to forty shillings – this had been paid in 1331.

In *'The History of Barnoldswick'* Warner states that; *In 1340 we find a Roll bearing the strange date 'May 32' at Westminster: - - -*

Inspeximus and confirmation of letters patent' of Queen Isabella granting to the abbot and convent of Kirkstall all tenements then in her hands within the bounds of the manor of Bernolfwyk in the counties of Lancaster and York.

But a Roll dated May 16th, 1342, is an exemplification of a writ bearing the date 26th June 14 Edw. III. (1341), commanding the bailiffs and foresters of Queen Isabella to permit the abbot and convent of Kirkstall 'to have without impediment certain tenements in the counties of York and Lancaster lately recovered against the King and the said Queen by judgment of court as pertaining to the manor of Bernolswyk Co. York.'

The legal proceedings had dragged on over the space of thirteen to fourteen years. And at the end of it all, and in spite of the judgment delivered in favour of the Abbey, the royal plunderers seem to have kept their prey. For in 1374 we find the following among the Fine Rolls:-

48 Edw. III. May 13. Commitment to the Abbot of Kirkstall by mainprise of Hugh de Wombwell and Walter Toppeclyf of the county of York - of the keeping of 100 acres of pasture in Admergill, late of the said abbot which have been taken into the King's hands for certain causes by Richard de Radclyf escheator in the county of Lancaster.

And so the tug-of-war continued. By 1374 the Crown had condescended to return Barnoldswick to Kirkstall with the proviso that it retained 100 acres of Admergill. As was the case with most records appertaining to land transactions we are at a loss to know exactly which area of land is referred to when looking at the above Fine Roll. However, we have the advantage of the 1580 map and this provides us with an insight into the landholdings that have been lost for centuries.

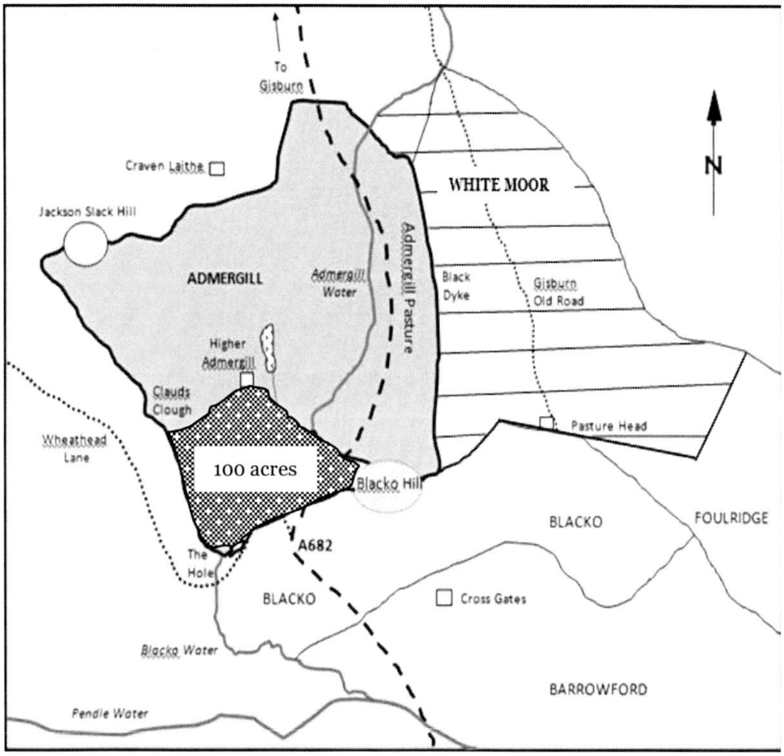

The 100 acres of Admergill retained by the Crown stretched from Higher Admergill Farm to Blacko Hill

Gills and Gateways

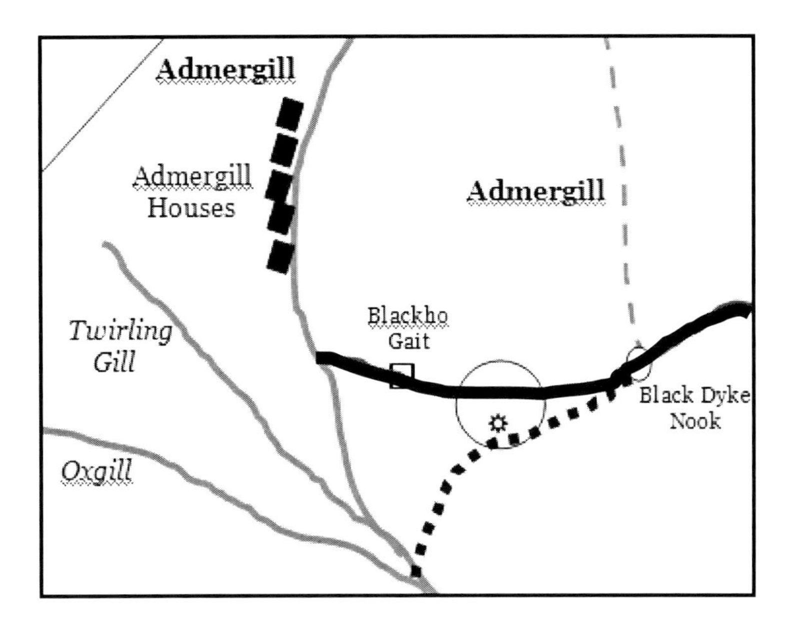

The 1580 map boundary is shown by the heavy black line while the dotted line represents the de Lacy boundary which corresponds with the pre 1974 county boundary line.

Blacko Tower stands on the apex of the hill today and this shows the extent to which the hill has been quarried.

It can be seen on the plan above that the White Moor Map boundary does not correspond to the boundary that Henry de Lacy traced over Blacko Hill in 1147. This has only recently come to light when we noticed that the angle of the boundary from the Black Dyke Nook to Admergill Water on the map made it impossible for it to be that of de Lacy's perambulation. This means that the Admergill estate, as portrayed on the 1580 map, is different in some respects to the estate that we see today. From the end of the Black Dyke the boundary of the map follows a ditch that is now difficult to trace. It ran between what is now Blacko Tower Farm and Blacko Hill and can only really be seen as it approaches the A682 Blacko to Gisburn highway.

The map shows the line of the boundary to run straight through the centre of Blacko Hill and this is why this line has previously been mistaken for the present ridge-top boundary. However, when we consider that during the eighteenth and nineteenth centuries the Blacko Hill was heavily quarried on the Admergill side the line of the map boundary begins to make sense. Half of the hill has disappeared, leaving a somewhat sheer northern face, and this means that the 1580 map boundary originally followed over the top of the hill.

We have seen that the map boundary is now difficult to trace on the higher hill slopes but things change dramatically lower down. From the A682 down into Admergill Water the boundary takes the form of a deep, wide gill. There is no mistaking this feature as having been an important boundary in the area; measuring some sixty feet in width in some parts the very size of the gill means that it could have been nothing less than a defensive boundary. Or could it? Well, we shall see later that there is strong evidence for there having been a defended settlement within Admergill and this gill would almost certainly have formed the northern defensive ditch. It can be seen that the map shows a feature called Blackho Gait straddling the boundary and fieldwork shows that this still exists. This is the spot where a major trackway from the west passed through Admergill and onwards to Gisburn and Barnoldswick. The track passed through the gill where the stream had been forded and a number of massive stones still lay scattered around the crossing. These once formed a defensive gateway across the gill through which the movement of people and animals could be strictly controlled.

Looking down the boundary gill into the Admergill valley and up to Wicken Clough (SD 855 426)

In an earlier statement on the naming of Admergill I argued that the Admergill Water valley is too wide to carry the appellation of gill. Given the size and location of this boundary gill I would further this by stating that I would be surprised if this feature were not to be the actual gill within Admer-gill. This is a very impressive earthwork whose purpose was almost certainly to control entry and exit along the valley of Admergill while at the same time acting as a formidable defensive ditch in times of danger.

Looking up the gill past the A682 highway to Blacko Tower.

The gill becomes shallower as it climbs the hillside toward the Black Dyke until it becomes difficult to trace. This face of the hill is all that remains following large-scale quarrying operations in the 18th and 19th centuries

The author at Blacko Gate.

This was an ancient crossing from one district to another. The original heavy gateway stones are still scattered around the area.

Another ancient gateway crosses lower down the gill the foundation gatestones of which remain in situ. The photograph does not truly illustrate the mass of these stones. Worked stones can also be found here suggesting that gateway of some status once stood here and, in all probability, this gill crossing would have preceded the higher one of Blacko Gate

This type of inter-district gateway is now extremely rare due to the fact that, over time, they became isolated as new tracks and roads began to serve the farms and land. Within our district I know of only two others, both within Pendle Forest. The largest one by far survives purely because its sheer size precluded its removal by successive generation of farmers at Rigg of England Farm. A large monolith acted as one of the gateway stones and remains in situ, set within a ditch that forms the boundary between the forest parishes of Higham and Old Laund Booth. A number of other massive stones have been cleared from the gateway and now lie unceremoniously in a heap nearby.

The remaining gate post at Rigg of England once formed a controlled access across the boundary of two Pendle Forest parishes (SD 818 378)

The gateway at Rigg of England shared a situation with the Blacko Gate in that it was situated on the ancient ridgeway route running from the west coast area through to Yorkshire and the east coast. Both, then, were placed to control important highways running through the district while also serving to act as defensive sites where the movement of people could be monitored, perhaps taxed and certainly prevented.

In what period, then, might these gateways have been erected? This is a fair question but impossible to answer as no archaeological methods can help with the dating of these features. It is fair to say, however, that the gates would be of a Medieval date at the latest. The two extant gates were situated on the ridgeway route that follows over the backbone of Pendle Forest and onwards to the east; finds of traded tools strongly suggest that there can be little doubt that this route was of importance within pre-history, from the Bronze Age at least. There is also every reason to believe that the boundaries upon which both gates sit were demarking territory within the Anglo-Saxon period (place-names and pre-Norman records show this) and so it is probable that the gates were being used for their original intended purpose from a latest date of c. AD 680.

Would there have been sufficient traffic through our area to warrant strong border points within the pre-Saxon era? We are given to believe (mainly from a lack of *official* archaeological evidence) that within the pre-historic era our district of Pennine East Lancashire was a backwater of little consequence. Consisting of a scattering of small, transitory settlements our pre-historic forebears would have had little need for gated routes. While I would argue with this in that we have far more evidence of large, stable settlements dating from pre-history (albeit unchartered on any archaeological survey) it seems reasonable to suggest that our pre-Roman settlers would not have seen a sufficient volume of traffic as to erect manned gateways. Our area fell within the pre-Roman kingdom of the Brigantes and within this northern hegemony were separate dependant principalities overseen by members of the ruling elite. It is possible that these were all singing from the same hymn sheet, so to speak, thus negating any need for strong defenses between the districts of the kingdom.

We know that the Romans found it necessary to control the conquered populace of England by using pre-existing Iron Age hill forts and erecting new defensive stations. Would the Romans have found a need to gate the route through our area? There is no doubt that they did indeed upgrade some of the roadways that traversed our district, the nearest official Roman road runs a mile or two to the north of Admergill where, on its route from Rimington, it passes by Todber and through Coverdale. However, these roads were intended for the efficient long-distance movement of men and goods, not as defended routes between local areas.

The early Medieval period following the fifth century withdrawal of the Roman authority left a native populace of Romano-British who could no longer be described as purely Celtic. There was already a power struggle blowing in the wind and the danger to the natives came in the form of the Angle and Saxon mercenaries invited by the Romans to help them to control the country. Of course, when the Romans left the Anglo-Saxons had no intention of leaving with them and so the face of England began to change forever. Again, though, there is no reason to think that our Pennine district held a sufficient populace to justify a Saxon military operation here. Indeed, it is unlikely that the Saxon settlers arrived within our area much before AD 680.

This leaves us with two possibilities when it comes to dating the erection of the gateway strong-points. The Saxon stewardship of the country took the form of a long and bitterly-fought series of campaigns during which large tracts of the country see-sawed between different noblemen. The coming of the Scandinavians saw the Saxon crown paying them off in the form of Danegeld and this resulted in our Pennine district becoming a part of the northern Viking territory of Northumberland. In the later tenth, and early eleventh centuries this was to change when the Saxon crown eventually subdued all of its enemies and united England beneath one king. Our area then transferred to the extended Wessex district of Mercia whose northern boundary became the River Ribble. During the protracted periods of Viking/Saxon conflict (during the tenth and eleventh centuries) our subject area became firmly set within a corridor of military activity. Being close to the lowest Pennine crossing point we attracted Viking incursions from both coasts, from Ireland in the west and York in the east. The Saxon Crown ordered that a series of defensive *burh* mounds be erected at strategic points and thus we have a period within which it would make good sense to erect strong gateways across our east/west highway.

Eventually things settled down and it is probable that the new Scandinavian settlers who arrived in our district settled relatively quietly upon lands not already settled by the Saxons, and not occupied by the remnants of the native British people who would have been here from at least the Roman Iron Age. The peace was not to last long, however, as the Norman invasion brought with it another hegemony with a need to firmly stamp its authority. The Normans erected their own series of burhs in the form of motte and bailey defenses, often adopting the Saxon mounds that had been well placed for the Norman purposes of controlling the people. The new castles and manorial centres were designed to subdue the surrounding districts and thus create a compliant workforce within the strict Norman feudal system. Here, then, we might see another period within which there had been good reason to erect our gateways.

This, perhaps, is the best we can say at present. There can be little doubt that there is significance in the fact that the Blacko Gate controlled a boundary that once separated two powerful religious houses (Kirkstall and Whalley), two counties (Lancashire and Yorkshire) and two powerful family seats (de Lacy and Percy). It also separated the two parishes of Colne and Brogden and Crown land from abbey land. Before leaving the subject of the gates it might be worth mentioning a record found within the Clitheroe Court Rolls appertaining to the Blacko Gate;

> ***1549****: Suite for ways between Lower Barrowford and Blacko:*
>
> *Bernard Hartley, Lawrence Hartley, James Hartley and Christopher Hartley, James Hartley of Fulshaw, James Hartley of Blacko, Lawrence and John Hargreaves, Lawrence Robinson, James Mitton and Lawrence Wilson versus Henry Bannester gent, Nicholas Smith and Christopher Robinson.*
>
> *The Jury ordered a sufficient way to be kept between Almys Kiln to a gap called* ***Out Gait in Blacko*** *on the land of Henry Bannester, Christopher Robinson and Nicholas Smith. Also a sufficient way from everyone's Doles across Stone Edge, along a hedge against Nicholas Smith's land, to the King's highway. Also Lawrence Hargreaves was to have a way at Short Clough Foot to the King's highway.*

We see in this record perhaps the earliest existing reference to the Blacko Gate (the *Out Gait*) and this continues through the Court Rolls where numerous land transactions in the Blacko portion of Admergill show this area as *Out Blacko*. The three land owners of *Henry Bannester, Christopher Robinson and Nicholas Smith* were being ordered by a jury made up of their peers to maintain the road between the Alms Kiln (near to the present Bridge Inn in Higherford) to the Blacko Out Gate in Admergill. Henry Bannister, of the Barrowford Park Hill family, owned the Higherford land to Whiteyate (now Whittycroft) and this joined Christopher Robinson's lands within the Stone Edge estate. From the Stone Edge boundary (around Beverley) Nicholas Smith was tenant of the Out Blacko lands stretching to the gill at Admergill within which we find the B*lacko Out Gate*. The road in question was not actually the one forming the modern A682. In 1549 the road ran from Park Hill, along the eastern riverside to the kiln near to the Bridge Inn, up the 'Brigg Hill' to Higher Whittycroft Farm, along to Stone Edge and then to the Cross Gates from where it branched and followed around Blacko Hill to Admergill.

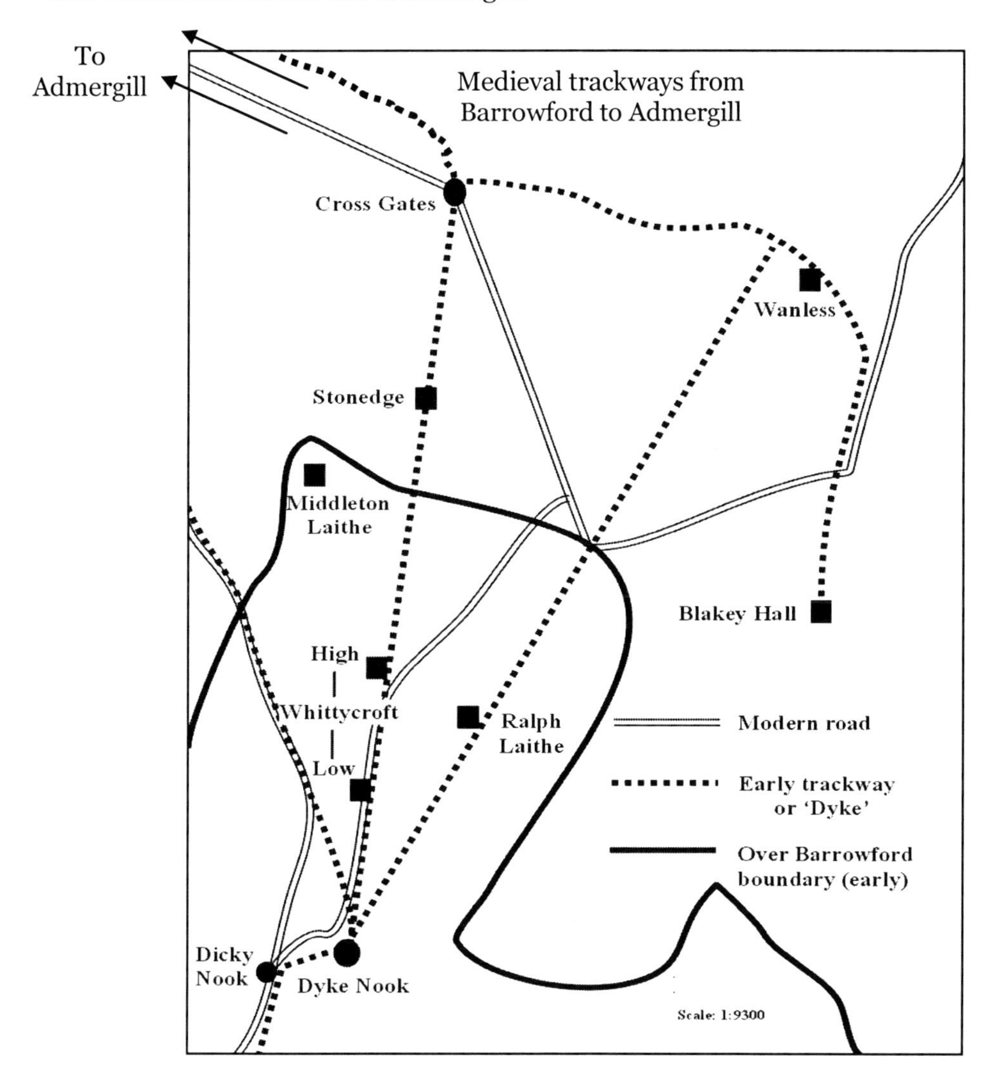

Chapter Four

Admergill: Vaccary and Village

The landowners recorded in the sixteenth century Court Rolls were the latest in a long line of tenants to have held their lands of the Clitheroe lordship. The Forest of Pendle was largely given over to farming by the de Lacys around the middle of the thirteenth century and this began an intake of waste lands that would transform our countryside from scrub and moor to the rolling green acres that we see today. The forest areas of Blackburnshire had probably been set aside for hunting purposes soon after the Conquest; these were the districts of Pendle Forest (between Pendle Hill and Ightenhill), Trawden Forest (between Colne and Boulsworth) and Rossendale Forest (between Haslingden and Cliviger), between them these districts formed almost one quarter of Blackburnshire.

We begin to see a formal system of forest records appearing within the twelfth century, by the year 1200 the de Lacys were keeping cattle in Rossendale Forest. However, the original usage of the forest areas as deer hunting grounds was still paramount at this time. The thirteenth century furnishes an ever-increasing volume and quality of record for the forest operations and surviving accounts for the later years show the farming methods, income, expenses and profits engendered by the Clitheroe estates. By now the importance of the deer had declined in favour of farming and the former forest areas were increasingly being turned over to cattle. This was a far more profitable use of the land and Henry de Lacy, having seen the success of a similar change of use in the Honour of Lancaster, embraced the new system of vaccary wholeheartedly.

By the thirteenth century the Pendle Forest district was dominated by cattle rearing through the establishment of the purpose-built *vaccariae* cattle ranches. The vaccaries gave rise to some very characteristic landscape features and settlement forms, which can still be recognised in the modern landscape. The centre of a vaccary was essentially a hamlet with several dwellings and associated farm buildings clustered together. The settlement was often in a girdle pattern round the arable area and footpath and bridleway evidence often points to a long-established focal point, the vaccary centre or headquarters.

The site of the vaccary was largely governed by topography, often (but not exclusively) the settlement would be sited in the valley bottom and the arable land lay behind the settlement to maximise the light available for crop growing. Low-lying vaccaries had at least one stock funnel or drift-way where animals were taken to, and brought down from moorland. These stock funnels tended to have curving boundaries which allowed for the more controlled movement of animals, especially the heavy draught oxen that were bred on the local vaccary farmsteads.

The settlement form of the vaccary has been the subject of only one archaeological investigation within the Pendle Forest area where at Sabden Fold (the site of the Goldshaw Booth vaccary) structures were uncovered, but with little dating evidence. To meet an increase in demand for food, as the population expanded during the thirteenth century, areas of former forest were cleared and waste land (known as *assart*) was brought into agricultural production. Not only was there a demand for more grain from the land but there was an incremental increase in demand for oxen to work the land. It was quickly realized that cattle rearing was far more profitable than game keeping, the cattle could be sold for draught, some were kept for breeding and dairy production and all eventually supplied meat and hides. Furthermore, in a district where valuable corn crops did not grow easily the cattle provided a welcome monetary return from the land.

By 1305 there were eleven vaccaries in Pendle Forest, all owned by the de Lacys who employed as their head cattle man one Gilbert de la Legh, of Hapton, who was an ancestor of the Towneley family. De Legh had his headquarters in the Accrington district and it was here that the central pool of oxen was organized within the forest areas. Beneath the head man (the chief instaurator) there was an instaurator in charge of each forest district. There were also horse breeding activities and the deer were not completely forgotten as breeding animals were transferred between the de Lacy estates in other parts of the country and venison was supplied as an on-going business. To this end two deer parks had been established at Ightenhill and at Musberry in Rossendale (along with a smaller one at Fence) and, by and large, it was here that the deer were confined. Henry de Lacy ran his vaccary system in Blackburnshire as a purely domanial operation (for his own use) and it was by far his largest enterprise within Lancashire.

We know that the monks of Fountains Abbey, and then Kirkstall Abbey, had control of Admergill within much of the period between the de Lacy grant of 1147 and the middle of the fourteenth century when the Crown retained 100 acres of land there. It was common practice for religious houses to farm their lands intensively, especially where the production of wool was paramount, and to this end they were not averse to slinging the inhabitants of monastic lands out of the area. This 'depopulation' was an unfortunate fact of life for the poor within history, those living in villages within official forest areas were also summarily resettled outside of the forest bounds, as happened at Higham within Pendle Forest.

To what extent, then, the estate tenants of Admergill were affected by the new owners of their lands in 1147 we do not know. Their former existence beneath a relatively fair Saxon noble (Eadmer?) would have seemed a very long time in the past. They had become serfs within the feudal overlordship of the new Norman regime and, no doubt, had been commandeered to dig some of the miles of ditches that surround the district. Then along came the Cistercian monks to Barnoldswick and with them a change of landlord.

Records tell us that the Barnoldswick parish of Brogden (to which Admergill was assigned) was depopulated about this time and we can only guess whether a hamlet existed at Admergill, with the consequence of removal of its inhabitants by the monks. It is possible that one, or both, of the monastic houses erected a grange at Admergill from which centre they would farm the district. Certainly this would have made sense given the distance from here to the original settlement of the monks at St. Mary's Mount in Barnoldswick. Having seen the records showing that the lords of Clitheroe were fond of encroaching onto the Barnoldswick moors with impunity it is not difficult to picture the scene: the monks at Admergill lived in a timber-framed grange house from where they ran a few hundred sheep on the moors and, every so often, a hunting party would pass their house with the chief forester of the Crown riding in all his finery at the head. Paying scant regard to the sour looks of the monks the hunters would carry on up the valley and thence on to the moors in search of their prey – probably oblivious to a few of the braver holy men who would angrily wave their sweaty sandals and curse the intruders.

By the latter quarter of the fourteenth century things had changed. The monks were finding that they controlled an ever-decreasing area of Barnoldswick, eventually being confined to a small area around Coates. Elsewhere in the country the population was reaching the end of a devastating century in which many of their number had died through a protracted period of famine and disease. Nationwide, the movement among landowners was from the growing of crops to the keeping of livestock and so it proved in our Pennine uplands. Tenants were now beginning to see an increase in their security and they paid their rents in cash, rather than in service to the lord. The Clitheroe lordship encouraged the intake of waste land into grazing land and a larger area was taken into the Pendle Forest vaccary system. And so, in 1397, we find that Admergill had officially become a vaccary within the Clitheroe estate and had been granted to one William de Radcliffe (son of John).

A *Compotus,* or annual estate account, of 1296 shows that Henry de Lacy's farming operation at *Barouforde* brought ten shillings per annum in rent. However, by the time of Henry's death in 1311 the usefulness of the vaccary enterprise was waning, the formerly high rental income from his vaccaries had been superseded by an income from rental profits. By 1324 only twelve of the vaccaries within the whole of the four Blackburnshire forests held the stock actually owned by the Honour of Clitheroe and even these were partly let out to tenants.

In 1323-4 there were three vaccaries in Barrowford (within which township Blacko and part of Admergill fell): one in Over Barrowford (Higherford), one in Nether Barrowford and a close of land at Blakey (Blacko). Simon de Blakey held one in Barrowford (at a rent of twenty-eight shillings) and this was based roughly upon the Fulshaw/Ridge area. John the Parker, of the Alkincoats family, had the other (at thirteen shillings and four pence) and this was the area north of Park Hill to the Blacko boundary. The close of Blakey was tenanted by Richard de Marsden (at twenty shillings) running from Blakey Hall down to the Barrowford boundary with Parker's vaccary. The higher lands of Blacko had not yet been taken into cultivation (officially at least) and the agricultural status of Admergill is unclear.

However, we see in the above record of the Radcliffe grant that the 100 acres of Crown land at Admergill had become an official vaccary by 1397 and we can begin to form a picture of the site at that time. The vaccary districts were split into booths (from *botte* meaning the rights and privileges appertaining within common law to the holding of a tenancy) and each booth would consist of at least a dwelling of sorts to house the stockman and his family along with some form of shelter for the stock.

Disease caused the highest loss of stock, murrain accounting in 1295-6 for as many as *'three or four calves of the year'* per vaccary. Over the whole of the de Lacy estate eighty *'calves of the year'* were lost, as well as ten cows. Within the generic term of murrain it is possible that we are seeing outbreaks of foot and mouth, rinderpest and pneumonia but it is also possible that murrain described all cattle diseases. Foot and mouth disease, like brucellosis, is one which leaves surviving animals with a degree of immunity but it remains endemic in a herd and will continue to cull young animals. Pneumonia in particular was commonly found in housed stock and this meant that a policy of the vaccary estates was to re-site the cattle houses on a regular basis. The expenses shown in the de Lacy estate records for 1295-6 and 1304-5 relate to *'removing and rebuilding'* housing for various classes of stock.

The cattle sheds would be of a prefabricated nature where upright timbers were easily fitted to roofing timbers by means of removable pegged-tenon joints. The thatch of bracken could easily be removed and burned while the woven wicker hurdles filling in the wall-panel spaces were re-used. It was a straightforward job, then, for a small team of workers to dissemble the building, remove the timbers and hurdles to a new site and reassemble it. This meant that the stock would be housed on clean, disease-free ground on a regular basis before bacterial infection could build up to dangerous levels. The expenses incurred for re-siting the building amounted only to new thatching and labour.

So, by the early fifteenth century we have an idea that Admergill would have had a central hall or farmstead in which the chief stockman and his family would live; this would probably not be William de Radcliffe (who was the chief tenant) as he would have been far too grand. Around his house the chief stock-keeper would have had a garden and an enclosure outside the wooden-paled garden would have held pigs and poultry. Somewhere nearby would have been a barn in which hay and corn was kept and oxen would occupy a separate bay. Here also would have been kept the communal plough along with the yoke and harness with which the oxen team pulled it. There would have been a dairy attached to either the house or barn and a workshop where timber was prepared and leather work carried out.

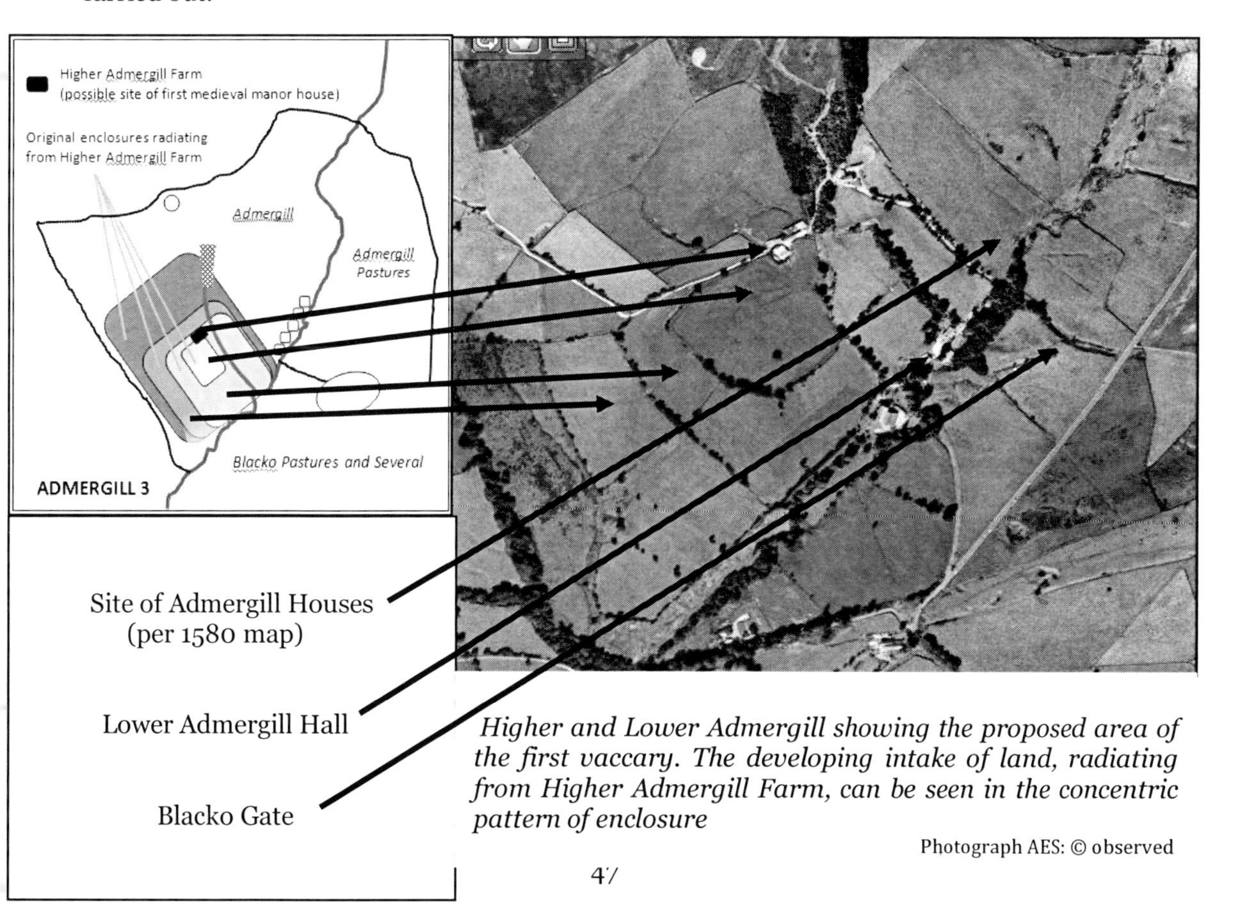

Higher and Lower Admergill showing the proposed area of the first vaccary. The developing intake of land, radiating from Higher Admergill Farm, can be seen in the concentric pattern of enclosure

Photograph AES: © observed

In the aerial photograph (previous page) a distinctive pattern of field boundaries can be seen. These indicate fields taken into cultivation at different periods and are typical of an expanding agricultural unit. The plan shows that the first cultivated area appears to adjoin Higher Admergill Farm and from here outer enclosures have been added in a concentric pattern thus providing the best agricultural land on the whole of the Admergill estate. This area corresponds with part of the proposed area of 100 acres that the Crown retained in the fourteenth century. The suggestion here is that we are seeing within this expanding intake of land the original extent of the Admergill vaccary granted in 1397. Further to this there is every possibility that this land previously formed the core of a Saxon agricultural unit and became the centre of a grange occupied by the religious houses. The site of the present Higher Admergill Farm, therefore, could well have been the original hall forming the core of the estate.

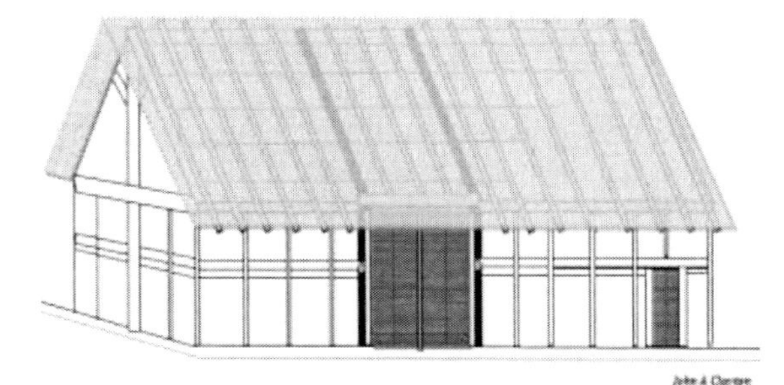

An impression of how a Saxon, or early Norman hall at Admergill might have looked

Further to this we saw earlier that the 1580 Map of White Moor shows a row of houses near to the boundary gill running down into Admergill and these have formerly been taken to have occupied the site of the present-day Lower Admergill Hall. However, having now located this boundary precisely it is possible to say that these houses represented a lost hamlet. An inspection of the area represented on the map as Admergill Houses shows that a settlement almost certainly existed two fields to the north-west of Lower Admergill Hall (photograph right).

Fieldwork in the area of the settlement shows that the Admergill Houses site occupies a field running to approximately seven acres and the area of probable inhabitation extends to around three acres. Aerial photographs of the site indicate that the whole of the field has been ploughed at some stage and the owner of the land confirms that it was ploughed during the war effort of WWII. On certain photographs it is possible to make out crop marks in the form of linear enclosures.

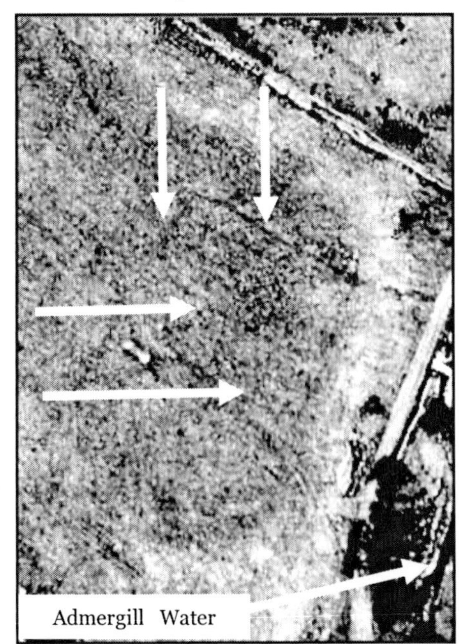

Mounds of proposed occupation correspond on the ground to the Admergill Houses marked on the 1580 map. The photograph shows crop marks on the site that appear to form the outlines of buildings

The proposed settlement site of Admergill Houses

Admergill Water runs to the extreme right of picture; the wooded area on the upper left is Wicken Clough. A sharply defined banking marks the site where the row of houses are marked on the 1580 map; a series of raised 'occupation mounds' mark the probable location of the individual houses (SD 855 427)

This series of crop marks covers the exact location of the Admergill Houses on the 1580 map and a 'keyhole' trench was put in over the return of an inner rectangle within an outer rectangle. This is a typical feature where a building stood within an enclosure and it was hoped to uncover the corner of any building here.

The soil was found to be of sandy consistency with a great deal of glacial rubble throughout. The top soil extends to around 60 centimetres beneath which the sub-clay level is reached. At a depth of 25 centimetres (the apparent limit of the plough depth) a stone much larger than the natural surrounding rubble (50 x 30 x 2.5 centimetres) was uncovered and consequent digging showed this have been one of a series piled one upon the other. The fourth stone in this series lay at a depth of one metre and proved to be too large to extract without extending the trench. Time constraints meant that discretion was the better part of valour at this stage and the trench was refilled. Due to the limited size of the assessment trench it was not possible to place this column of stones within any particular context. They are not coursed and neither was there any mortar present but it can be said that they were not within a natural context and therefore indicate the hand of man. There were also fragments of pottery within the waste from the trench, most of which lay at a depth of around 10 to 20 centimetres. The depth, however, cannot be taken as any indication of how long the fragments might have been within the soil as in all likelihood the plough would have continually churned them to the surface.

The top of the pile of stones (left) at a depth below the ploughing level. The fourth stone (right) was too large and deep to be removed within the constraints of the exploratory dig.

Also within the trench was evidence of the return of a rubble wall where the upper layer had been removed by the plough. The constraints of the trench size meant that this could not be verified.

Successive to the dig a quality metal detector was used to assess the whole of the seven acre field in the hope of locating 'hot-spots' of settlement material. The area of proposed habitation was by far the most productive in this respect. Although no firm dating evidence came to light the area of the proposed 'occupation mounds' turned up a concentrated cluster of ironwork relating to settlement. This took the form of a smith-made leather punch, numerous hand-made nails, hinges and large iron nail-bolts. Only a fraction of the iron targets were actually recovered from the 'occupation' area due to the high concentration of non-ferrous material but it is fair to say that the percentage of finds removed from the site is indicative of human activity here. As the field climbs the slope towards Wicken Clough the incidence of ferrous objects lessens markedly. The only finds higher up the slope, and away from the level site, were brass fittings from nineteenth century agricultural machinery.

There is, of course, always the possibility that the occupation mounds formed a tipping area for dwellings elsewhere but the fact that there are five of them, all evenly spaced across a strip of elevated land along the riverside, would suggest otherwise.

Pottery finds within the extended site appear to date from the Medieval through to the Tudor periods and this fits nicely with the Tudor date of the 1580 map.

Pottery from the extended area of proposed settlement.

*Example **A** appears to be Medieval while the black-glazed earthenware in **B** could be Tudor.*

On the riverbank, around 50 metres above the site, there is a rectangular stone-flagged area, measuring approximately seven metres by four metres. A single stone step leads onto this platform and the thickness of the flagstones (7.5cm) suggests that it supported machinery or was designed for some other industrial use. Around this site the metal detector found a large quantity of slag material consisting of large, heavy lumps of burnt material within which shards of pottery are embedded.

This suggests that a kiln or furnace operated here, the obvious inference being that it was either a grain-drying operation, a pot kiln or a blacksmith's shop. This latter is a strong possibility as a small, enclosed circular close of land adjoins and access to the enclosure was through a gateway immediately adjacent to the site. This raises the question as to whether this site contained a smithy for general ironworking duties, including the shoeing of oxen and horses – the enclosure would have been ideal for holding the animals to be shod.

The 'smithy' site (single black arrow) is located close to the Admergill Houses site (double black arrows) with an adjacent enclosure on the stream bank (white arrow)

One of the Medieval gate posts leading from the 'smithy' site into the adjacent enclosure

An ancient ford crosses the stream of Admergill Water bringing a trackway directly into the proposed settlement of Admergill Houses. Another track runs along the western boundary of the site field and this once ran onto the moor top with a branch forking across to Higher Admergill Farm. From the ford any traveller leaving the proposed settlement would have headed along a hollow-way up the steep slope towards Blacko Hill. This track still exists and can be seen to take the form of a stock-way where animals were taken up onto the higher pastures and brought back down to the valley via a meandering route, the reason for which was two-fold. Firstly there was the obvious advantage of a series of bends that would alleviate the strain of a steep climb and secondly a herd of cattle could be more easily managed on a steep downhill slope because they had to negotiate sharp bends.

Looking south across the Admergill Houses site into the valley bottom and up to Blacko Hill

The copse within Wicken Clough is right of picture and the curving stock-track is indicated (black arrow) as it leads down from Blacko Gate (white arrow) to the ford

A study of the trackways within this part of the Admergill estate shows that the modern road that delves down into the valley from the A682 at Blacko Bar is a relatively modern one. Originally the trackway indicated in the above photograph would have been the main route into the proposed settlement via Blacko Gate from the western approaches. A track served Higher Admergill Farm by running along a course from Blacko Laithe straight down and across Admergill Water and up the other side – the line of this can still be made out.

The tenants living in the hamlet shown on the map as *Admergill Houses* would almost certainly have been subservient to the chief stockman living at Higher Admergill in the post-Norman period of vaccary farming. It is also possible that a settlement on this site could have had its roots within the Saxon period and the tenants here would have been tied within the Saxon manorial system.

Although this image is obviously contrived it does provide a very rough portrayal of what the Admergill Houses might have looked like in the late Medieval - Norman period. The houses here are sited on the proposed occupation mounds within the site.

The Medieval ford gateway still remains (above)

The stock-way crossed the ford where the tree stands (right)

Hopefully we are now getting a clearer picture of the history of Admergill; we know that within the post-Norman Medieval period there was constant conflict between the three parties of the Crown and the religious houses of Fountains and Kirkstall for control of the estate. Eventually, by the latter quarter of the fourteenth century, Barnoldswick had been returned to Kirkstall Abbey by the king who kept for himself an area of 100 acres. This probably covered the whole of the cultivated lands of Admergill stretching from the boundary ditch over the Blacko Hill ridge to Higher Admergill Farm. This area of Crown land was considered to have been part of the royal land holdings of Pendle Forest within the Clitheroe lordship within Blackburnshire and, therefore, within the parish of Colne within the parish of Whalley.

The extended Admergill estate was part of Blacko which, in turn, was part of the township of Barrowford and bordered the parishes of Roughlee, Wheatley with Barley, Burn Moor, Greystone Moor, White Moor, Pendle Forest, Rimington Moor and the Craven district of Yorkshire. Admergill was part of Colne parish for the payment of poor rate but part of Barnoldswick for the payment of church tithes. The estate remained within the constabulary of Yorkshire, was a detached part of the Barnoldswick parish of Brogden but fell within the jurisdiction of the Lancashire court holdings of Ightenhill. Confused? So was everyone else!

As an illustration of this we see that in 1688 Thomas Parker, a Colne worthy, wrote a letter to Justice Roger Kenyon at Preston stating that:

> *The inhabitants of Colne Parish design to move the Justices, at the Sessions at Preston, for an order to cause the inhabitants of Admergill to contribute towards the relief of their poor; by what law or rule, the writer does not understand. They neither being in the same parish or county!*

Admergill valley viewed from the slopes of Green Bank.

Far left is the Moorcock Inn, on the A682 Blacko to Gisburn highway

Chapter Five

Other Sites within Admergill

Before we take a tour of the other ancient and historical sites within Admergill it is worth mentioning that the opinions put forward within this text are done so without the benefit of professional Archaeological research. This is the reason why the *proposed* lost hamlet is not given as fact even though fieldwork and research of maps and records show the existence of such a site to have been a probability. It is hoped that at some stage within the near future the importance of Admergill as a highly preserved depository of our colourful history will be recognised by those bodies with funds and expertise enough to do the site justice.

That said, let's press on. From the following it will be seen that Admergill has a number of features, all of which have the appearance of holding an important place within our local history. It must be said, however, that the sites that are offered below are the ones *that I am aware of* - this is by no means intended to be a comprehensive survey of the estate. There is little doubt that further research would uncover more evidence of occupation within Admergill. The plan below (**Admergill: 4**) shows the location of the sites covered in this text; we have already seen the *Admergill Houses* in the lower half of Site C and *Alainseat* in Site H.

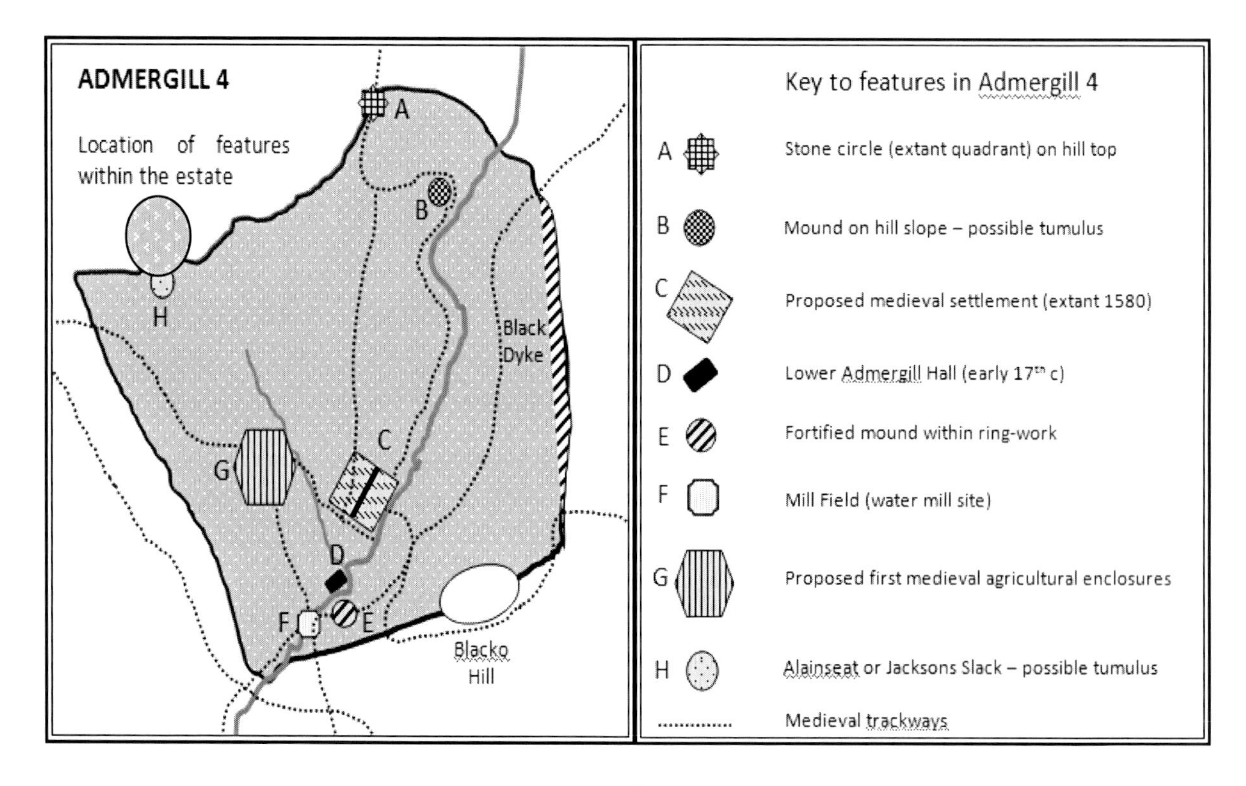

Beginning at the logical point of **Site A** we find ourselves on the level area atop the Green Bank (SD 856 433). This is the steep, bracken covered hillside that faces directly towards the Moorcock Inn on the A682. The site is located on the very edge of Burn Moor and straddles the modern boundary between Admergill and Greystone Moor. Here, on the Admergill side, we find a large marker and, within metres of this impressive, flat-topped boulder, there can be found what are almost certainly the remnants of a stone circle. The vast majority of these 'ringstone' monuments were cleared from moorland and scrubland during the many periods within our history when the pressure for increasing amounts of agricultural land caused the clearance of everything that stood in the way. In this way we have lost known stone circles at Spen Brook, Ringstone Hill (Shelfield, Nelson) and Ring Stone Hill in Barrowford (Water Meetings area).

That said, there were limits to the size of stones that could be uprooted and dragged to the hedgerow (or rolled into the nearest stream) by a pair of oxen or farm horses. Many of the stones found within ancient monuments have come to resemble icebergs in that over ninety per-cent of their bulk has been buried with the encroachment of millennia. This means that the largest and most obstinate of the monument stones can still be seen in situ (where they have not been buried altogether). And such is the case with **Site A** where the tips of four buried stones can be seen on the Greystone Moor side of the wall. These can be seen to have formed a quadrant that can be extrapolated into a forty-five metre diameter circle extending into the Admergill side of the wall.

On this side of the wall it can be seen that the stones that once completed the circle have been removed from their original positions and piled so as to form the base of the modern enclosure wall. These particular stones are of a manageable size and were obviously no problem for the people who enclosed this land, probably in the early part of the nineteenth century. It would not be too strong a flight of fancy to suggest that these stones would form an impressive landmark when still in situ and they could, therefore, have been the *grey stones* that gave rise to the name of this area being called Greystone Moor.

LEFT: Looking up Green Bank to the level top where the stones of ***Site A*** *are located.*
RIGHT: Three of the four stones within the quadrant

These large wall-stones probably once formed part of the circle but were not too large to be moved when the moor was enclosed.

The area of **Site A** is not alone in holding a number of large stones; the extended hillside here has many examples of massive stones that could not be uprooted. The side of the hill was quarried on a small scale during the time of the moorland enclosures in order to provide stone for the new walls. This left a couple of circular pits to scar the side of the hill but it is unlikely that the large stones scattered across the area were related to this quarrying operation. Many of these stones lie above the quarries and have the appearance of having lain undisturbed for a very long time.

One of a number of almost-buried boulders on the Green Bank hillside.

We can only guess as to the actual size of this stone were it to be excavated

Two more examples of the large stones that lay on Green Bank

The proposed stone circle at ***Site A*** *is marked here by an arrow. The ellipse denotes the extended area containing a scattering of large stones and the two small quarries*

As to dating the proposed circle, this is impossible without the aid of archaeology. Any datable evidence that might be found within the context of this site is hidden beneath the peaty soil and will remain so until such times that the site can be properly investigated. As a final word on **Site A**, in the 1970s I saw a stone embedded in the surface of the ground within the ellipse shown above. This stone was roughly square and measured about fifty centimetres across; on the surface was carved a symbol strongly resembling a rune. Despite a search in recent times I have been unable to locate this stone again, despite the fact that the landowner (who also has seen the stone) has given me directions. Given the tendency of the memory to play tricks I cannot state definitely what shape the symbol took; I have an image of a candelabra with two or three arms similar to these: ᚠ ᛉ

There is also a possibility that the symbol was carved for fun by a quarry worker in his tea-break! Unfortunately that is all that can be said until the stone is found again and the symbol can be identified.

Moving from the level at the top of Green Bank we can follow the quarry track as it traverses the steep side of the hill. As the track reaches the bottom it comes hard up against a very large earth mound. This is **Site B** and I have to admit that this feature could be anything; it is possibly a drumlin left after the melting of the ice-cap some nine or ten thousand years ago. It could be a spoil heap where the waste from the quarries above was dumped. It could be just one of nature's little banana skins placed there to make the landscape historian look foolish – or it could be a burial mound.

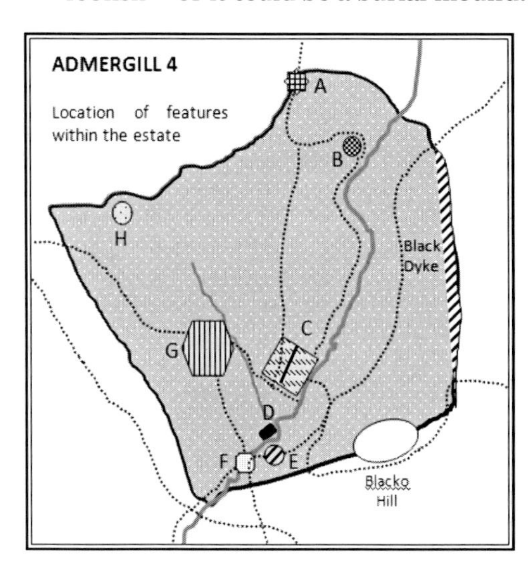

To address the above possibilities, the mound sits hard against the bottom of the steep hillside and stands out because no other features of this type exist. Over millennia the Admergill Water stream has washed this hillside base in times of flood and consequently the valley base sweeps smoothly up to meet the hillside along the whole of the Admergill valley. This particular mound is sharply conical in shape and this suggests that it does not sit comfortably as a purely natural feature.

*The mound (arrowed) at **Site B** sits hard against the base of the steep Green Bank hillside.*

There is a good chance that the mound is indeed a spoil heap, the fact that it is located at the very bottom of the trackway leading up to the quarries is a strong indicator of that. There is, however, a point in that material from the mound would more than fill the quarries and therefore it contains too much material although the spoil could have been dumped on a lesser mound that happened to be on the site. If the feature turns out not be a burial mound then the quarry waste theory must be a live contender.

If it so happens that we are looking at a burial mound here then there is the obvious question of which period it might belong to. Archaeological evidence should quickly answer this but in the meantime we can only surmise that any burials within the mound would date from the Neolithic through to the Saxon period. The valley bottom siting of the mound might preclude an early date, the Iron Age culture especially tended to place their tumuli high on ridge tops and hillsides where they were obvious to others and made a statement. There is a possibility, then, that any burial here would be from the Saxon period. If this turned out to be the case then we could be forgiven for thinking that within the mound-casing lies a burial of some note – perhaps the Saxon thegn, or minor prince, who owned Admergill many centuries ago?

To the edge of the mound top is a large mark stone; this could have been moved within antiquity but does appear to have been related to the mound. Of all the sites considered within this book it has to be said that this particular one is the most likely not to have been created by the hand of man - whatever the case, without proper investigation we will be left guessing at the origins of this mound forever!

Moving westwards along the valley we pass the Admergill Houses at **Site C** which will be seen on the plan **Admergill 4** to have been separated into two roughly equal halves. This denotes the lower site of proposed settlement and the higher section of the field in which a very interesting artefact has recently been uncovered. We saw earlier that this field was ploughed during the 1940s and it might very well have been put to the plough at other times during the past 400 years. In fact we know that the Admergill Houses were depopulated at some stage after they were shown on the 1580 map and this could have been as a result of the landlord requiring the site for arable use.

The boundaries of **Site C** consist of an ancient trackway to the west, an ancient ditch to the north and a ditched banking to the west, this latter having been formed by a wall of large boulders. Towards the top of the field we recently found a very rare example of a stone bowl-quern which, in all probability, had been long-buried before being hit by the plough at some time. As was the common practice the quern was removed from the path of the plough and dumped in a ditch.

These quern stones were used for grinding corn, herbs and pigments by the use of a hand-held rubbing-stone. In the Admergill example the base of the stone has been purposely shaped so as to be set in the ground and secured so that the grain could be ground in a circular motion until it was refined enough to be used as flour. The more common type of quern was the elongated *saddle quern* where the rubbing stone was used in a to-and-fro motion thus creating a long, flat shape as opposed to the bowl shape. It thought that the bowl quern dates to a period before the middle of the Iron Age as the rotary (or beehive) quern became the standard type of quern from this period onwards.

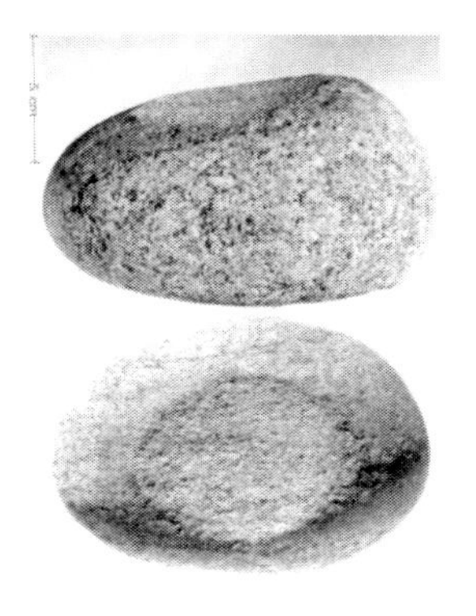

The Admergill bowl quern with a type of rubbing stone (inset)

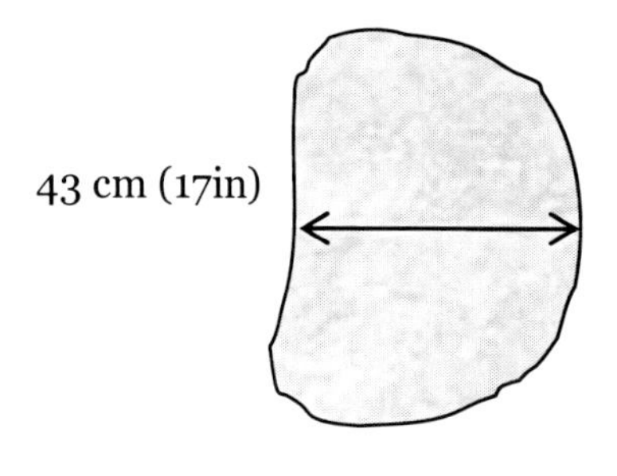

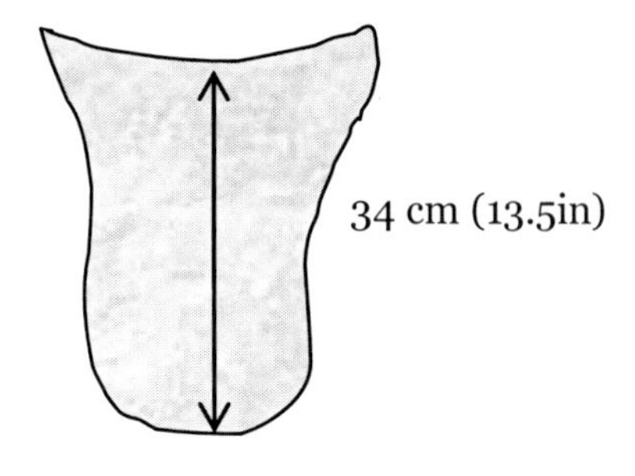

The *rotary quern* consisted of a flat slab base with a wooden dowel set into the centre around which a hollowed upper-stone rotated. The grain was fed into a hole in the top of the upper-stone and this was rotated against the base by means of a handle, the ground grain spilling out at the sides.

The rotary quern represented white-hot technology at the time of its introduction to Britain (about 400-300 BC) and would have been at the top of every prehistoric housewife's shopping list. Before this time saddle and bowl querns were the standard method of grinding. This, then, would suggest a date for the Admergill bowl quern of not later than the middle of the British Iron Age and possibly much earlier than that. This, in turn, suggests that the upper part of the field in which the quern was found could well have been an area of pre-historic settlement. Further to this, it does not require a giant leap of faith to place this find within context to both the postulated stone circle at **Site A** and the postulated tumulus of Alainseat on the moor directly above the quern find at **Site C.**

Chapter Six

Admergill Defences

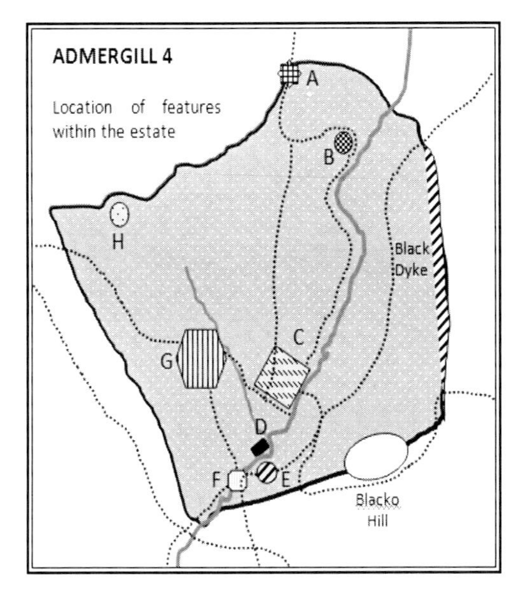

Leaving **Site C** we pass Lower Admergill Hall by the riverside track and begin the climb up the access road toward Blacko Bar. About a third of the way along this minor road we come to **Site E** and what is possibly the most impressive feature within the Admergill estate. Here we find an elevated mound surrounded by a pronounced ditch (or ringwork).

The mound has been created by digging a deep ditch around it and piling the spoil into the centre; because the site occupies sloping ground there would have been much less labour involved in raising the mound than had it been on the level. An obvious trackway leads from the lower part of the site and wends its way around the mound banking on to the top. Here the mound top forms a level site of 30.5 metres (100 feet) in diameter.

The mound (arrowed left) looking from Admergill Water. The track is marked by the right arrow.

To assess the mound in **Site E** it is necessary to take a wider view of the site in relation to the extended area of East Lancashire and Yorkshire Craven.

The main point to consider at this stage is the strategic location of Admergill; although there are very few defensive archaeological sites marked on the maps of our area this does not preclude the existence of far more. To further this argument we know that the hill fort at Castercliffe (on the heights above the town of Nelson) was what it says on the tin because we have the benefit of archaeology to tell us that it was in use as a defensive feature up to a date of around 600BC. Furthermore the impressive mounds, ditches and earthworks at Castercliffe (or Tum Hills as it is known locally) somewhat give the site away as an ancient feature to anyone who cares to take a close look.

In this vein we can see other sites within our landscape that might not have the benefit of archaeological provenance but are, nonetheless, almost certain to have been defensive sites. We find such a place on the riverside at the Barrowford Water Meetings (SD 854 410). I have been proposing this site as a settlement to anyone who will listen for a number of years, the reason for my conviction being based on fieldwork and map work. The site is a raised level area .5 kilometres in length and .25 kilometres at its widest point. The whole of the site is enclosed by banks, ditches and streams; the southern boundary being Pendle Water while the northern limit is formed by Blacko Water. The eastern approach has been heavily fortified by means of a series of ramparts and ditches through which the road from the east/west ridgeway runs. This site, then, was highly defensible; it is washed on two sides by waterways and had a large, level enclosed space that would hold a sizable settlement. It was also placed directly on a major route.

The Water Meetings site looking west through the rampart earthworks from Pendle Water

There can be little doubt that this site formed an area of defended settlement and was possibly contemporary with the hill fort at Castercliffe. Two Iron Age tracks led from this latter site; one passed down Botte Lane, through Swinden, around the southern end of Rye Bank at Barrowford, over the barrow-ford and up to the ridgeway above from where it could take the traveller westward, northward or eastward where it followed through Utherstone Wood and down to meet the track through the Water Meetings site. The Rye Bank at Barrowford is the long bank of land forming the backdrop to the park and is the 'barrow' in Barrow-ford. Again, this area of raised land would have been an ideal place for a defended settlement, surrounded as it is on three sides by almost sheer embankments. Again we find that it was situated on major routes from Castercliffe and Pendle Forest.

Barrowford Rye Bank

Castercliffe hill fort

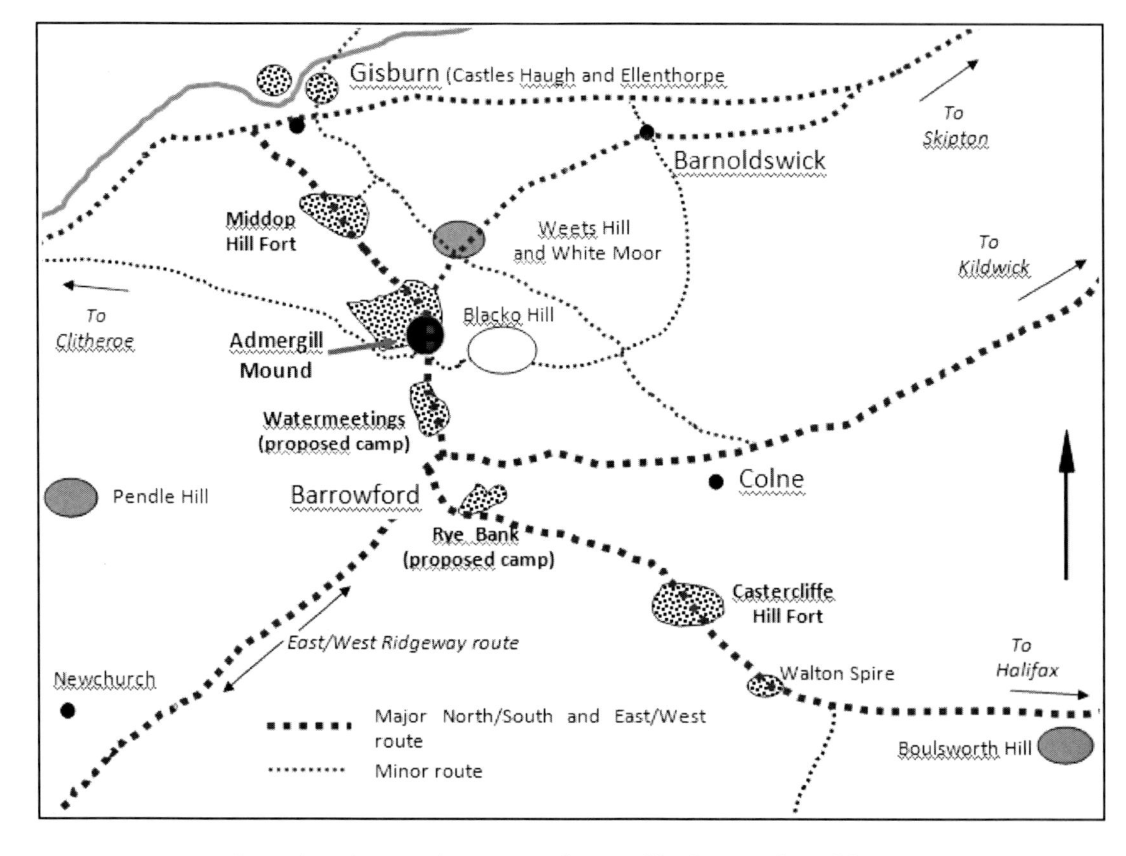

Plan of ancient major routes denoted by heavy dotted lines

Lower ramparts of the Middop hill fort

The plan above shows a further three defensive sites; the earthwork at Middop is situated a mile or so down the valley leading from the head of Admergill down to the River Ribble. This is one of the most impressive ancient hill forts in the north of England (pictured left) and, to illustrate my point on the lack of *official* archaeological sites within our district, it remained (and still remains) largely unknown until historian Stanley Graham, of Barnoldswick, pointed it out to us. The trackway from Admergill led through this site and joined with Coal Pit Lane on its way from White Moor to the Norman castle mounds on the banks of the Ribble at Gisburn.

Here, then, can be seen a line of defended sites running coterminous with an arterial route and it can surely be no coincidence that the Admergill mound at **Site E** is placed directly on this former highway. From the (proposed) Water Meetings site the track from Castercliffe followed along to Blacko Foot, along the side of Blacko Water to the ford at Wheathead Foot (now the '1914 Bridge') and over a (still extant) clapper bridge spanning Claudes Clough to the north bank of Admergill Water. Here it followed along the north bank of Admergill Water and an eighteenth century estate map shows there to have been track (or gateway) called the Oastgate and this possibly referred to the trackway along the Admergill beck. Having reached Lower Admergill the track crossed the stream near to, or at, a point where a clapper bridge of indeterminable date now stands. From here the trackway climbed to the mound by entrance between two ridges forming a gateway through which any traveller could be monitored.

This clapper bridge is sited at the Medieval crossing point from Lower Admergill to the mound and onwards to Gisburn and Barnoldswick.

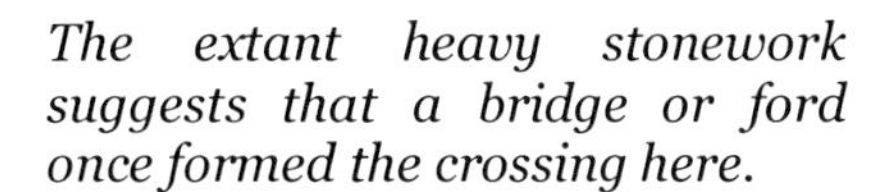

The extant heavy stonework suggests that a bridge or ford once formed the crossing here.

The mound and ditch have been placed in a highly defensive position with the sheer banking of the stream forming the western side. The stream takes a ninety-degree turn when it has passed beneath the clapper bridge and this creates a steep drop from the mound on its southern flank. Immediately to the north a deep gulley runs from the ridge of Blacko Hill down to the site, where it forms an excellent defensive ditch, and drops into the stream below. The photograph above shows the point at which the track leaves the mound and crosses this gulley.

LEFT: The trackway from the ford leading to the top of the mound

RIGHT: Looking across the ditch and tracks to Lower Admergill Hall centre right

The first defence on the northern side of the mound site is a deep gulley.

The mound within **Site E**, then, is proposed as a defensive site where it would have enabled strict control over the movement of people from the Yorkshire district who would have travelled up the Middop valley and into Admergill. Equally any traffic from the east would have passed through the mound site.

Now, the perennial difficulty here is in the establishment of a date for the creation of this (proposed) fortification. The temptation is to ally the mound site with the creation of the massive gill nearby to which I have ascribed the appellation of the *Admer Gill*. This latter can surely be nothing other than a control mechanism within the landscape whose purpose was to delineate the enclosed/settled land while stopping undesirables from gaining entry therein. This form of enclosure has been employed since time immemorial and the gill could, therefore, have scarred the Admergill landscape for thousands of years. However, before the weight of millennia can be ascribed to the gill it must be remembered that there have been innumerable occasions within our long and colourful history where the inhabitants of an estate such as Admergill would wish to keep the riff-raff at bay.

Fair enough, the Admergill mound is situated directly across what once served as a major trackway contemporary with the Iron Age hill fort of Castercliffe. It is also fair to say that this trackway would have been in use well into the Early Modern period. This, then, allows plenty of scope within time for the erection of a defended mound. To fast-forward from the period around 600BC, when Castercliffe is thought to have been abandoned, we arrive at the Roman era but, as was argued earlier, there is no evidence for there having been a strong Roman military presence within our district.

There is an argument for the post-Roman British to have defended against the incursions of the Anglo-Saxons and, were Admergill to have originally been a British settlement, then it would not be the greatest of shocks. After all, we know that there was a native presence hereabouts from the Celtic place-names – a local example being found at Utherstone Woods above the Water Meetings site. The Brithonic Celtic word *udd* meaning *great*) could well be the first element within *Uth*-er-stone; could it also be the first element within *Ad*-mer-gill (*great boundary gill*)?

Again, we are severely hampered by the lack of archaeology on **Site E** and can do little other than surmise through the use of guesswork based upon best available evidence. And so, with this in mind, we could bring the dating of the mound much closer to our own period. We have already seen that one of the major upheavals to have affected our forebears was the Saxon struggle against the Scandinavians. This was not a single all-out battle, as appears to have happened at the tenth century Battle of Brunanburh. The conflict was continual for centuries and within the Wessex versus Northumbria power struggle were many other minor conflicts where local Saxon thegns and nobles fought their neighbours for local control of land. Many of these minor noblemen built their own small defended settlements, sometimes in the shape of stone or timber tower strongholds and sometimes in the simple form of a moated hall. At this stage this origin for our mound cannot be precluded.

Once the Saxon crown had taken a firm grip over the whole of England they had little time in which to consolidate before the good-old French arrived and with them another round of upheaval and fortification. We see at Castle Haugh (photograph below), in Gisburn, an example of a Norman motte where a mound (possibly a former prehistoric burial or Saxon burh) was fortified by placing a wooden structure on top. The castle was erected in the eleventh century as part of the Norman defence system designed to assert control over the conquered people and to defend against uprisings from the north.

The striking Norman motte mound of Castle Haugh at Painley (Gisburn)

This site is very similar to the mound site at Admergill in that it took the form of a ringwork created by a dry ditch (two metres deep) around most of its circumference. Castle Haugh also used the sheer banks of the river as its defence along one side of the defended site. The mound was also placed across a major route that connected with the trackway through Admergill – in this way, then, the two sites were connected through design and an obvious purpose of controlling the same thoroughfare through the Pennine gap.

As far as our quest for a reason, and a date, for the Admergill mound goes we could have a contemporary site in Castle Haugh. We have seen that the Normans erected this latter defence as a stronghold to enforce the stewardship of the Norman fee in Cravenshire. This was a normal state of affairs where the new hegemony doled out the former Saxon estates to their cronies. Now, to illustrate where I am going with this in respect of the Admergill mound it is necessary to take a quick look at the state of the political climate surrounding the people of Admergill at this time.

Following the Norman Conquest events began to unfurl that would culminate in the creation of the historic county of Lancashire. William I was faced with problems of insurrection from his noblemen in the North and regularly had need to march on York to reassert his authority. On the 20th September 1069 a faction of the army of Swein, king of Denmark, joined forces with a group of English rebels, amongst who was Earl Waltheof, and the coalition captured the city of York. They demolished William's castle there and slaughtered the resident French garrison. William understandably took umbrage at this and for the third time that year found himself on the long march north. He was determined to stamp out the insurrection once-and-for-all, having bought off the Danes he set about wreaking a destruction that must have been horrendous to behold. Everything within his path to York was ravaged, villages were burnt, crops destroyed and livestock killed. An eleventh century writer stated that:

> *Never did William such cruelty; to his lasting disgrace, he yielded to his worst impulse, and set no bounds to his fury, condemning the innocent and the guilty to a common fate.*

This *Harrying of the North* was truly shocking; never again did the north think to oppose William. It is known that his destruction was carried out north of York but it is not clear as to what extent he ravaged Lancashire. The Domesday Book mentions that of the fifty-nine vills dependent upon Preston '*16 of them have a few inhabitants . . . the rest are waste.*' There are a number of possible explanations for this however; other than destruction at the hands of William it is possible that the area had not recovered following the ousting of Earl Tostig, the former controller of the district, in 1065.

The upshot of all this was that William decided that he needed a hard man to take charge of his naughty northern subjects and he decided upon Roger de Poitou, the third son of William's cousin, Roger de Montgomery. Thus in 1071 Roger de Poitou was entrusted with the huge north-west estates of lands between the Ribble and Mersey (Lancashire *south of the sands*) and large holdings in the Craven district of Yorkshire. Here we can see a period where there was good reason for the erection of small castle sites within our region. Castle Haugh was built on Cravenshire lands about this time, Barnoldswick fell within Cravenshire and Admergill fell within Barnoldswick. Although the mound at **Site E** formed part of the Clitheroe estate we are looking now at the period when it was considered to be within Barnoldswick. This raises the possibility that the two sites at Admergill and Gisburn, so similar in position, size and design, might well prove to be entirely contemporary.

By the year 1086 the king had reclaimed the Lancashire and Cravenshire holdings for the Crown; the reason for this is unclear but was possibly due to a rebellion or a land exchange. By the 1090s Roger de Poitou again held the Lancashire estates along with the lands north of the sands. In 1102 Roger again lost the estates when he joined with his brothers in a rebellion against Henry I. Ilbert de Lacy acquired the honour of Clitheroe as a royal tenant (he had been granted the fee of Pontefract by William I) in 1102, having been placed as a reliable *Overlooker in the North* by Roger de Poitou, and it fell to this baron to oversee the defences of the hill country around the Pennine borders - the family retained the lordship for over a century. The lands were kept together as a unit and granted to Henry I's nephew Stephen, Count of Bologne (later to become King Stephen) between 1114 and 1116. In 1138 the Scots army occupied the areas north of the Ribble and Ranulf II, Earl of Chester, annexed the lands between the Ribble and the Mersey (our area included), eventually holding them legally between 1141 and 1149.

So, things were complicated following the Norman invasion. However, from the above scribings we see that one Ilbert de Lacy held the Clitheroe and Craven lordship from 1102 and this would have included the tenancy of Admergill which his brother Henry's descendant, another Henry de Lacy, handed over lock-stock-and-barrel to Fountains Abbey in 1147. Within Ilbert's overlordship were undertenants who were usually classed as knights, holding their lands of a *'knight's service'* where they had an obligation to provide military service to the lord (who in turn provided military aid to the Crown). These undertenants were in constant preparation for battle in that they retained small bands of armed men upon whom they could call when the need arose. These knights occupied houses of a higher status than those of their retainers and many of these houses were of a defensive nature. If the house, or hall, was not built as a defended site the knight and his retinue would live within the safety of an extended bailey overseen by the motte (mound) stronghold.

At this period, so close to the Conquest of 1066, it is difficult to find any worthwhile evidence to suggest who might have been the head-man of the Admergill estate. It is possible that a Saxon, who formerly held the land in thegnage, was allowed to retain Admergill as a working estate; albeit with the destruction of any hall or manor house within the enclosure of the defended mound here as the Normans would have destroyed most of the defended Saxon sites. Alternatively the new regime could have taken over the site and placed its own man at Admergill.

To continue with the theme of political complexity within the post-Norman invasion there are another series of events that might well have been related to our mound site at Admergill. Following the winter of 1136-37 King David of Scotland took advantage of the power struggle for the English throne between Stephen and Matilda and invaded England in a bid to take the earldom of Northumberland into his power. An army of northern English knights and their retainers were waiting for David's army at Newcastle but a truce was agreed until November. When the truce had lapsed David demanded of King Stephen that he forfeit the lands of Northumbria, naturally Stephen refused and David invaded England in the January of 1138. An English chronicler related that this invasion was brutal;

> *An execrable army, more atrocious than the pagans, neither fearing God nor regarding man, spread desolation over the whole province and slaughtered everywhere people of either sex, of every age and rank, destroying, pillaging and burning the vills, churches and houses.*

By February Stephen was bringing his army north to confront David but the two protagonists managed to avoid each other and Stephen, with the conflict for the throne uppermost in his priorities, headed back home. Following this David split his army into two and sent his nephew, William Fitz Duncan, to march into Lancashire, where he harried Furness and Cravenshire. On the 10th of June Duncan again met with a force of northern knights at Clitheroe where a pitched battle took place. David won the day and the English were routed but in the August the tables were turned at the Battle of the Standard near Northallerton. King David was granted the Northumbrian lands and thus he held control from the Tees to the Ribble. Eventually William Fitz Duncan inherited the Honour of Skipton-in-Craven.

And so we see yet another reason why the Admergill valley would have been considered to have been worth defending. We know that King David's army was active within our area in the earlier period of the 1130s and the Battle of Clitheroe shows that William Fitz Duncan was hereabouts with an army in 1138. There is a record of King David having destroyed a castle within Cravenshire when he invaded – was this the Admergill site? It is fair to say that it was more likely to have been Castle Haugh as we know that this was a definite castle site and was strategically placed on the very edge of King David's Northumbrian territories.

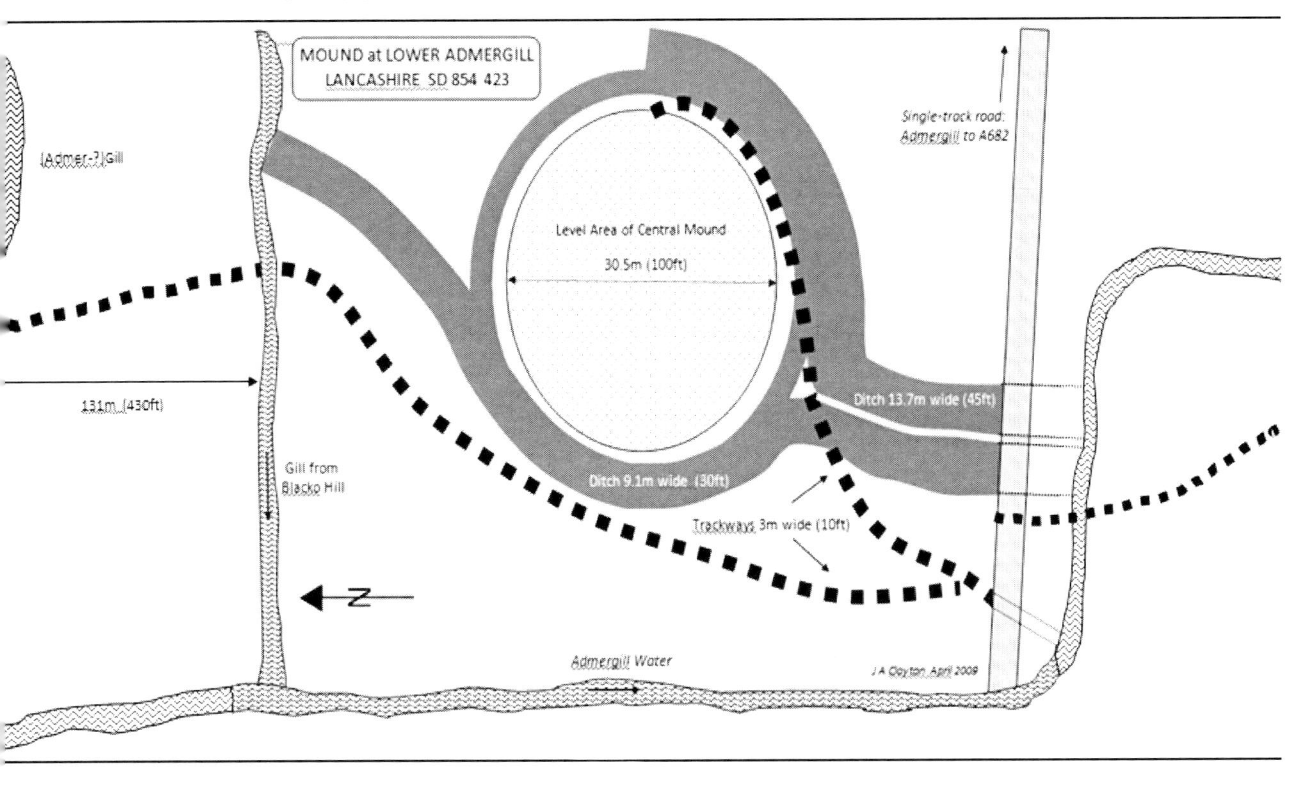

*Plan of **Site E***

The deep gill (Aedmer's Gill?) to the north, and the steep stream embankments to the south and west, form three highly defensive boundaries. The fourth boundary was possibly a now-levelled ditch to the east (on the Blacko hillside) or the Blacko Hill itself

Having looked at the protracted period of unrest that stretched from the tenth century Scandinavian incursions to the fourteenth century Scottish uprisings it is well to remember that the fears of the local populace did not end there. The townships of our area were in constant danger of raids from Scottish borderers long after Stephen and David's conflict had settled down. One of the reasons for this was the fact that Scottish inheritance laws meant that all male children inherited the lands of their fathers and this meant that a farm could be split many ways when there were a number of sons. A fifty acre holding could end up as five ten acre plots and this was not enough land to sustain the families of each son. As a consequence of this there were huge bands of disaffected young men who felt that their only recourse was to pillage and rob to sustain themselves. Some gangs of Scottish borderers numbered in the thousands and these groups were fond of heading south into

England to rustle cattle and anything else of value that they could lay their hands on. This state of affairs led to the erection of large numbers of fortified houses and towers throughout the Scottish border lands and down into northern England. This could have been the reason for the erection of the Admergill mound as the area saw a great number of Scottish raids.

Having reached the fifteenth century it is clear that the reasons for an estate such as Admergill to defend itself did not abate. We have seen that William de Radcliffe, the son of John, was granted the vaccary of Admergill in 1397. The Radcliffes were an important family whose seat was at Radcliffe manor near Bury. The original manor house at Radcliffe is believed to have been built in the late eleventh to early twelfth century by Nicholas de Radeclive and the surviving section known as Radcliffe Tower was a rebuild of the earlier manor house, built by James de Radcliffe (1355-1410) in 1403.

Radcliffe Tower is an example of a stone pele tower and, in order to fortify the building, James had to apply directly to Henry IV for a *'licence of crenellation'* and this was granted at Pontefract in August 1403. The list of crenellation licences shows that there were very few applications (granted) within Lancashire - Towneley and Gawthorpe keeping company with Radcliffe – and it is clear from the list that only the higher echelons of society were ever in a position to even apply for such a privilege. There can certainly be no suggestion, then, that Admergill ever held a building of sufficient status to render it of any real importance within the late Medieval society.

Hellifield Pele, Yorkshire.

This is a rare example of a fortified tower house within our district

If the arguments above hold any merit at all then we have to consider that any building on the Admergill mound would have been designed with defence in mind while forming the core of the Admergill estate. This could mean a timber Saxon hall within a stone and timber breastwork, surrounded by a ditch. Alternatively the mound could have held a Norman motte 'castle' in the form of a timber tower within a stone breastwork. Also, moated or ditched sites were often used by minor knights as status symbols and the early Norman tenants of the Admergill estate could have lived within the mound enclosure. There is another possibility, hitherto unmentioned, in that the 1147 grant of Admergill to Fountains Abbey could have seen the monks erecting a church, or defended grange house, on the site. Any church here would have been small and intended for the use of the monks and the immediate population as the Barnoldswick church at Ghyll served the Brogden parish.

Impression of how a Saxon hall on the mound might have appeared

There would have been a stone or wood enclosure around the breast of the mound

So, we have an obviously defensive mound with no other evidence of date, or specific use, than a cursory inspection provides. Again, we suffer from the lack of archaeological evidence and it is hoped that the short history above might at least not be too far removed from the truth. As a final word on the mound, examination of the breast-edge shows that a wall surrounded the platform although it is not known to what height. Furthermore, around ten years ago the landowner had need to excavate a small area in the centre of the platform to an approximate depth of 1.5 to 2 metres. Within the spoil from this excavation were found to be a number of heavy, worked square stones suggesting that any structure here was more substantial than if timber alone had been used. Further to this the gulley forming the first line of defence for the site contains a number of very large stones placed along the banking and it is not difficult to imagine that a very solid wall lined this feature. The gill (The *Admer Gill?*), which formed the outer defence also contains a number of massive boulders that would once have lined its banks. Most of these have been broken up and taken away over the centuries but the larger ones were rolled into the gill where they still remain as testament to an age of social upheaval.

Chapter Seven

Admergill Hall and Monastery

There is the question as to when any stone structure on the mound in **Site E** (be it curtain wall or building) might have been demolished and where did the stone from the site go? There is evidence scattered around the present-day Lower Admergill that early stonework has been used in conjunction with later building stone. Until around fifteen years ago the ruins of a building known as *The Monastery* stood to the west of Lower Admergill Hall (**Site D**).

The Monastery at Lower Admergill: early 20th century
Photograph courtesy of Stanley Graham

A nineteenth century photograph of The Monastery (my copy of which has been mislaid) shows what appears to be a sixteenth century building of three bays. There was originally a simple hall sited tangentially to the stream with the main entrance in the gable. A matching bay was later added and this shared the original entrance. There was no porch. At a later stage still a smaller cross-wing was added to the southern side and an outshut was built onto the northern side. By the time the building was demolished it had crumbled to the height of the lower window heads. In the photograph (above) it is apparent that the right-hand side of the building was a later, and poorer quality, addition. The original windows show fine tracery in the stone upper glazing heads. Both Higher and Lower Admergill houses contain remnants of The Monastery where large stone fireplaces and door lintels have been incorporated into the internal structures.

It can be seen in the photograph of The Monastery that the coursed stonework is somewhat irregular in size. The lower courses, as might be expected, are larger that the higher ones but the differing height and width of these suggest that were reclaimed. If this is indeed the case then this (probable) sixteenth century building was erected on foundation stones brought in from another site. Also, the dry stone walls surrounding the Lower Hall appear to be Medieval or Early Modern in date and contain worked square stones of the type evident within the base of The Monastery.

Many worked building stones are evident within the walls around Lower Admergill

Lower Admergill Hall: circa early 20th century

Photograph courtesy of Stanley Graham

*Lower Admergill Hall in 2009: **A** is the original Hall - **B, C** and **D** were the farm buildings*

The earliest surviving building on the Admergill estate is the Hall which is said to date from around 1611. At times this was referred to as The Hall while the Monastery was called The Old Hall. The extended building of what now constitutes Lower Admergill Hall shows at least three phases of construction. The original hall of c.1611 (**A** in the photograph above) was extended by the addition of **B**. The barn building **D** was possibly built in the eighteenth century and then had the farm house of **C** added at some stage. Building **B** would then have been added to fill in the gap.

In 1896 **B, C** and **D** were put up for auction along with 103 acres of land where the property consisted of the: *Farm House – Barn – Shippon – Stable – Yard – Garden – Croft at 3 acres: 0 roods: 38 perches*. The house and buildings were said to *'have recently been entirely rebuilt at considerable cost and upon the most modern principles.'* This, then, provides an apparent date for **B, C** and **D** of around 1896. It would be interesting to know if this is the date when the architectural features seen in **B** were added. The right-hand window lintel, and the left-hand window reveal, are not original and were taken from the ruins of The Monastery at some stage. The doorway in **B** has been formed into a window, again by using a massive reclaimed lintel. If these reclaimed features were to date from the 1896 rebuild then it is clear that The Monastery was being quarried for material at this date and would probably have been in ruins for many years prior to that.

Beside the farm buildings and croft the auction also included 103 acres, the whole lot bringing £103. The estate map accompanying the sale does not include what is now called Lower Admergill Hall - this belonged to the Trustees of Ms. Weldon. The field names and areas were given as:

1896 - Lower Admergill with Brogden:
From the deeds of the Colne Estate of Thomas Shaw:

Farm House – Barn – Shippon – Stable – Yard – Garden – Croft 3a or 38p
Cow Heys 3a 2r 5p
Mill Meadow 5a 2r 37p
Middle Meadow 5a 1r 31p
Far Meadow 7a 2r 34p
Football Ing (Site of Blacko village playing fields) 6a 12r 8p
Higher Heys (Heys = boundary) 9a 1r 2p
Lower Heys 4a 3r 31p
Wood Heys 0a 1r 28p
Plantation 1a 2r 16p
Hole Meadow 3a 0r 2p
Further Marles 10a or 34p
Money Gates Pasture (near to turnpike road toll house, Blacko Bar) 2a 2r 15p
Money Gates Meadow 2a 2r 7p
High Gates Meadow 6a or 7p
Part of Banks Pasture 6a or 7p
Part of Banks Pasture plus seven acre piece 14a or 26p
Holme 0a 2r 24p
Blacko Hill 11a or 20p

Total: 103 acres: 3 roods: 8 perches

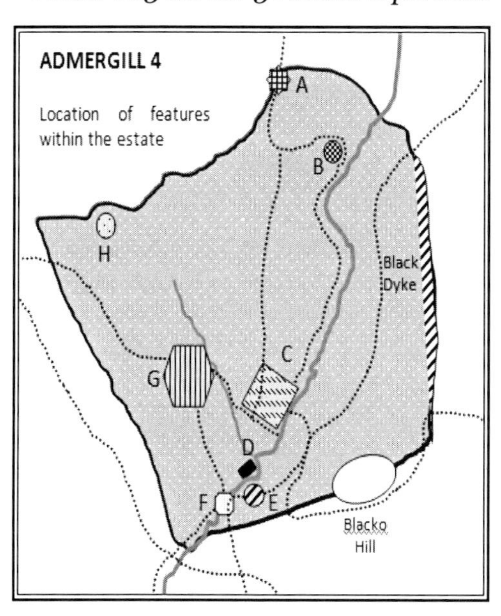

Admergill Mill

Site G on the **Admergill 4** plan represents the proposed site of the first vaccary at Higher Admergill and we have already covered this. The estate auction list above shows that one of the fields belonging to Lower Admergill Farm was known as Mill Meadow and this brings us to the final site in this tour of Admergill. The meadow is marked on **Admergill 4** as **Site F** and can be seen to adjoin the mound at **Site E**.

The Mill Meadow with Admergill Water on the right

We are on firmer territory with this site as we can be almost certain that there was a mill at Admergill from the evidence of the field name, the presence of grooved rack-stones incorporated into the walls hereabouts, and the existence of very large worked stones within the stream alongside the Mill Meadow. The questions arising here are what type of mill would we have seen here, exactly where was it and of what date would it have been?

Firstly, we can say that the mill was a water powered corn mill. The grooved rack-stones that survive around the site were used for the flooring of a grain drying kiln where grain was prepared for milling by means of an operation known as *'sieve and fan.'* There is no trace of the mill on this site on the early (1840s) OS maps of the area and so we can conclude that the structure had outlived its usefulness and been demolished by then - this would preclude the use of steam to power the mill.

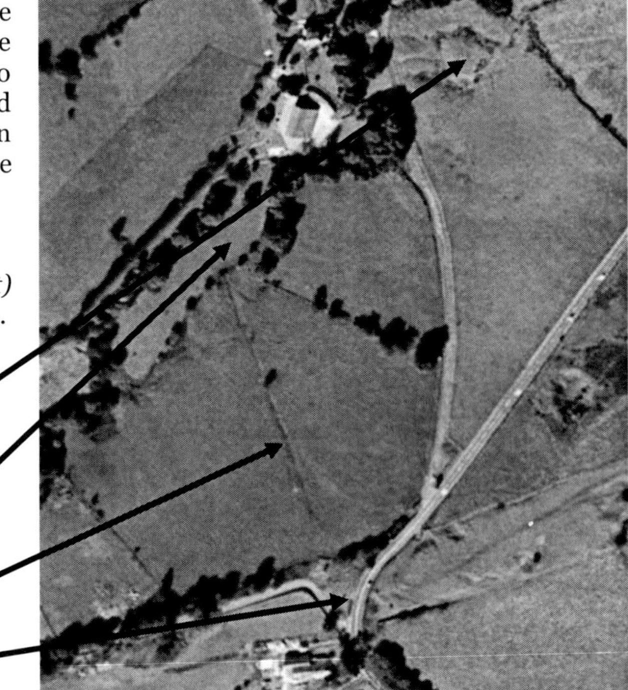

It is clear on the aerial photograph (right) that the Mill Meadow adjoins the mound site.
Photograph: Stock - AES Imaging – © observed

Mound

Mill Meadow

Track to mill from Blacko Bar

Blacko Bar

The problem, of course, is in locating the exact site of the mill and dating the period within which it operated. Before the modern road down to Lower Admergill was created the mound at **Site E** sloped directly down into the mill site and this suggests a strong link between the two. In fact it was common for defended manor sites to incorporate a water mill and this could be what we are seeing here.

Water mills formed an intrinsic part of any Medieval society and fell into the four distinct groups of **Royal, Monastic, Manorial** and **Pirate**. The royal mills were controlled by the Crown who extracted *multure*, or taxes, from everyone who used the mills. This meant that the mill sites were strictly controlled and usually operated only by those with a licence to operate them. There were, however, instances where mills were operated by monastic houses within their own hegemony (as might have been the case at Admergill) and others, more rarely, were operated as 'pirate' mills outside the control of the Crown.

The number of mills within a district depended upon the density of the local population in times of population growth there was a higher demand for crops and the subsequent conversion of those crops into flour. There is a possibility that the Admergill Mill was erected to serve the monastic grange community within the Brogden. At the time when a grange might have been established at Admergill there would have been only a limited population within the district to use its services and this suggests that any mill dating to that period would have been a small operation for the use of the monks. Certainly during the thirteenth century there was a sustained population growth nationally.

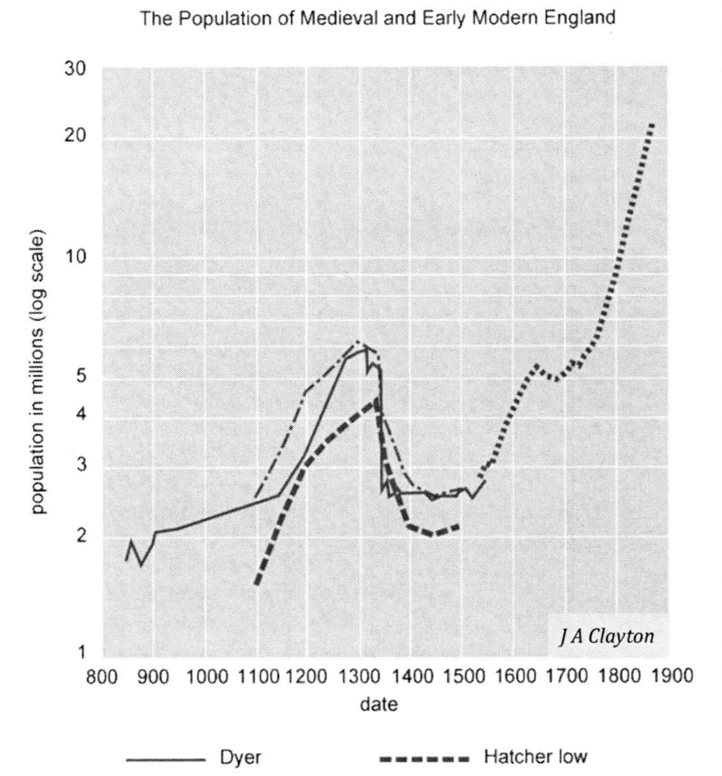

The population of England compounding the data from three different sources ie., Hatcher, Dyer and Wrigley and Schofield.

Taking this information it is clear that from c.1100 to c.1290 population growth was constant. However, there were still periods of crisis as the nature of things dictated that no century ever saw a continual annual crop yield of above average return (as illustrated in the table below).

Centuries	Number of Famines	Number of Years of Famine	Years of Famine
1001-1100	7	10	1004, 1005; 1042; 1069, 1070; 1073; 1086, 1087; 1093; 1096.
1101-1200	7	10	1111? 1124, 1125, 1126; 1162; 1175, 1176; 1183; 1189; 1196.
1201-1300	7 + 3	9 + 5	1203; [1205]; 1224, [1246, 1247]; 1252; 1257, 1258; 1271; [1286]; 1289, [1290]; 1294, 1295.
1301-1400	4 + 2	6 + 3	1315, 1336, [1317]; 1341; [1359]; [1363]; 1369; 1390, 1391.
1401-1500	+ 7	+ 8	[1401; 1416; 1434; 1439, 1440; 1486; 1491; 1497].
1501-1600	1 + 5	+ 9	[1521; 1545; 1557; 1574; 1587; 1594, 1595, 1596, 1597, 1598].

J A Clayton

Data source: William Farr: *Journal of the Statistical Society of London*, Vol. 9, No. 2. (Jun., 1846), pp. 158-174.

The period of growth within the twelfth and thirteen centuries corresponds with the grant of Admergill to Fountains Abbey and there could well have been a mill on the site at some time during this period. The year of 1290 saw the end of the long period of growth and things were to go steadily downhill from there. The country experienced a five-year period of famine and as a consequence the population began to fall rapidly. By the time of the arrival of the Great Plague in Lancashire (1349) the populace were at a low-ebb and were susceptible to the ravages of the disease. The population did not really begin to expand again until 1500 from which date we see a continuous decadal expansion through to the present day.

1575	-10	1585	-10	1595	-30	1605	20	1615	-5
1576	-12	1586	-44	1596	-85	1606	11	1616	-3
1577	-5	1587	20	1597	-65	1607	8	1617	-12
1578	13	1588	26	1598	2	1608	-38	1618	15
1579	12	1589	-2	1599	12	1609	8	1619	22
1580	0	1590	9	1600	0	1610	10	1620	38
1581	20	1591	28	1601	12	1611	-1	1621	20
1582	28	1592	32	1602	14	1612	-9	1622	25
1583	26	1593	12	1603	22	1613	-23	1623	12
1584	-10	1594	20	1604	15	1614	3	1624	10

Table of annual crop quality during the sixteenth century (relating to the average yield)

J A Clayton

Proportion of agricultural wages to the price of corn:
The League 1844

Period	Weekly Summer Pay (ex. harvest time)	Wheat per Quarter	Wages in pints of wheat
1495	2s:0d	6s:3d	163
1514	2s:0d	8s:8d	118
1545	2s:6d	18s:8d	68
1593	2s:6d	20s:0d	64
1610	3s:6d	34s:1d	52
1725	5s:0d	35s:4d	72
1750	5s:0d	29s:2d	122
1763	7s:0d	33s:1d	108
1770	7s:4d	41s:4d	92
1793	8s:5d	46s:9d	94
1824	8s:7d	64s:0d	68
1829	11s:0d	62s:1d	85
1833	11s:5d	55s:9d	104

The average worker's wages related to the number of pints of wheat they would purchase.

The lower amounts of the sixteenth and seventeenth centuries represent good crop returns when prices were higher.

There is a suggestion, then, that there would have been little reason to erect a mill in the Admergill backwater between the later fourteenth century (when the monks had lost control of the Admergill Mill site) and the early part of the sixteenth century when things began to pick up again. Further to this we know that there were royal mills operating within the district. In the early sixteenth century the Clitheroe Court Rolls record a deposition of local tenants who were pushing for the erection of a new mill in Pendle Forest because, as they said; '*the tenants of Blacko have to take their corn to be ground at Foulridge mill*' – this strongly suggests that there were no (working) milling facilities at Admergill during this period.

As a consequence of this deposition the mill at Carr (Barrowford) was sanctioned and this was erected about the year 1533; prior to this the tenants of Pendle Forest were obligated to use the mill at Bradley (Great Marsden). Another mill was built at Damhead, in Roughlee, in 1597, and this illustrates that the conditions in the sixteenth century were generally advantageous to the mill owners.

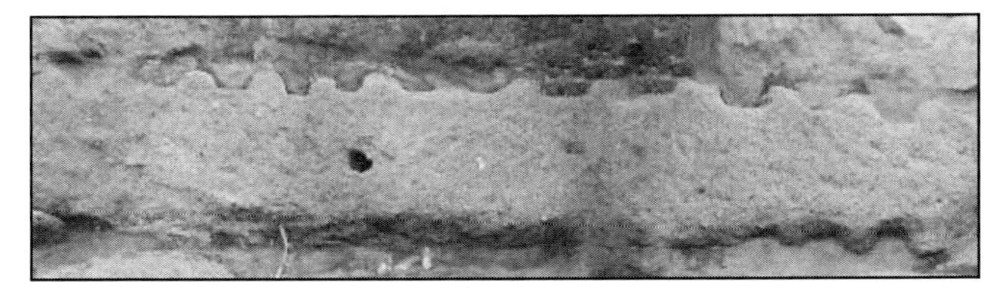

Grooved rack-stones embedded in buildings and field walls indicate the presence of a former mill or kiln site

The need for corn mills was given a boost in 1507 when the Crown instigated the official deforestation of the Pendle and Trawden Forests. The former tenants were allotted their holdings by the king and these were let by means of copyhold. This new security of tenure saw a rapid expansion in the number of farmsteads throughout the area as more land was taken into cultivation. This in turn meant an increase in local arable production and more demand for mills. This being the case the erection of the Admergill Mill could date to sometime between (say) 1540 and 1600. This is not to say that there was definitely no mill on the site before this – perhaps an earlier, abandoned mill structure was adapted and updated at this time.

The Admergill milling operation was unusual in that it does not appear to be mentioned in any of the Clitheroe Court Rolls. There are numerous references in the Rolls to other local mills, especially where people had withdrawn their multure (or *soke*) illegally as we see in the following Court record;

> ***1538:*** *John Smith of Over Barrowford, Christopher and John Robinson, Thomas Holt, James Hartley, Lawrence Blakey, Christopher Blakey, John Hanson, Christopher Nutter, John Hartley of Roughlee, Christopher Hartley of Roughlee, Robert Swire (the relict of Robert Blakey) etc etc. all fined 1d for withdrawing their soke from the Kingsmill at Colne.*

A point worth mentioning here is that at the time of the Pendle Witch trials (1612) Elizabeth Southern (Demdike) stated that she, along with her daughter, had; '*helped out Richard Baldwin's folks at the mill.*' Baldwin lived at Wheathead, in Roughlee, and came from a family of millers, one branch of which lived at Admergill. Now, Wheathead Farm is situated less than half a mile from the mill site and the streamside track (possibly called *Oast Gate* where *oast* = *kiln*) ran directly between them. The common assumption has always been that Baldwin's mill was the one at Damhead in Roughlee but this was almost three times the distance from Baldwin's home at Wheathead than the Admergill site, the inference being that local was always better as carting had to be paid for.

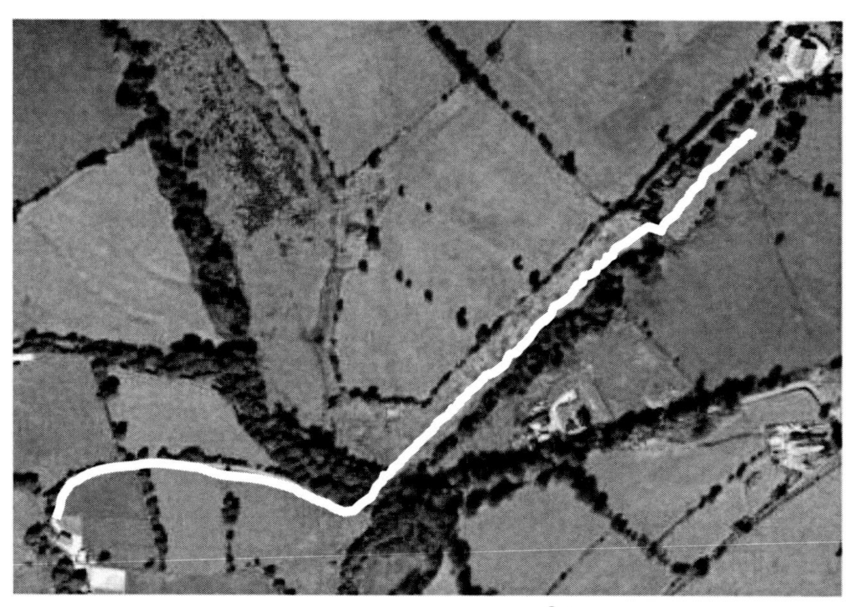

The short route between Wheathead farm and the mill site followed the Admergill stream before crossing by way of a ford

Photograph: Stock - AES Imaging © observed

In miller Richard Baldwin, of Wheathead, we see a man of the new order who had risen within society and carried some authority within the justice system. He was a Puritan, with jaundiced views relating to his poorer neighbours, and had the ear of Justice Roger Nowell of Read Hall. If Baldwin were indeed to have worked the Admergill Mill then we can see within his sphere of social contact that he might have been allowed to operate outside of the usual constraints of mill ownership and, therefore, his operation did not show up in the manorial records – in other words wheels within water-wheels!

However . . . this is unlikely. The rights of the mill owners were jealously guarded and a small pirate mill would have been no match for the gentry owners such as the Towneleys. To illustrate this there is a court record showing that in 1658 Christopher Towneley, of Carr Hall and Carr Mill, took a band of his retainers, armed with staves and clubs, and descended on Barrowford where they smashed the mill caul in order to disable the competition. The mill in question was that which stood on the land of the Bannisters of Park Hill (now Barrowford Park). Judged by his peers it is not surprising that Towneley escaped punishment!

Another point against Baldwin having used Admergill Mill becomes apparent when the manorial records for Foulridge are examined. Having seen that the township had been at loggerheads with its neighbours in 1580 (the reason for the existence of the White Moor Map) there was another major land dispute in 1594. Here we see an award made;

> *To Barnarde Towneley of Hurstewoode, gent., Robart Jackson of Worsthorne, and Christofer Bawdwen of Weethead in Pendle, yeomen, concerning disputes between lords and owners of Foulerygge over allotments and rebuilding of the mill.*

This would suggest that the Baldwins of Wheathead held shares in Foulridge Mill and would naturally have used that site for grinding their corn.

All-in-all the evidence begins to mount in favour of the Admergill Mill having been operational at an early period. It is clear that the sixteenth century would have been an optimum time in which to erect a mill but the lack of written evidence goes against a late Medieval mill site at Admergill. Were the mill here to have been working during the tenure of Fountains or Kirkstall then we would not expect there to be any particular reference to a small, backwater mill and, as far as I am aware, the abbey records do not mention any such activity.

The Abbott of Whalley rented lands in Blacko in the fifteenth century and, in 1536, Richard Baldwin paid a *'tithe for sheaves'* to the abbott at ten shillings and ten pence. This raises the possibility that Whalley Abbey were the owners and operators of the Admergill Mill so as to take advantage of the local corn production and convert it to flour in the immediate locality. This would also have the advantage of bringing in revenue to the abbey; furthermore it would explain why the largely non-secular Court Rolls do not appear to hold any reference to the Admergill Mill.

Another factor to be considered, where a site (such as a mill) performed a service to the community is that of social upheaval. We have seen that Christopher Towneley attempted to sabotage Barrowford Mill and this was not an isolated case. Other mill owners sabotaged the mills of their competitors but a greater threat was to become apparent in times of political turmoil. In the later fifteenth century the Wars of the Roses saw a great deal of unrest within our county border district and it would be no surprise if we were to learn that Admergill Mill had been destroyed within this conflict.

The sixteenth century saw Henry VIII break with Rome and the resultant destruction of the monastic system brought with it a land-grab of unrivalled proportions. Were Admergill Mill to have been held by the Abbey of Whalley then it could well have been closed, or destroyed, by order of Thomas Cromwell during the 1530-40s. Again, the Civil War period in the seventeenth century saw the destruction of many buildings.

On the 25th of October, 1569, the court for the manor of Ightenhill convened at Higham where Henry Towneley sold Carr Mill;

> *Henry Townleye, gent., surrendered, by Thomas Rylaye, a tenant of the Queen, one water corn mill in the Forest of Pendle called le Carre mylne with all the watercourses to and from the said mill and all the soke and suit of the tenants of the New Hold within the Forest of Pendle belonging the saide mill in any way, annual rent to the Queen 20s, to Thomas, son and heir apparent of Thomas Lyster of Westbie, esq., Richards Smythes, Lawrence Townly, gent., and John Harteley of Admergill, yeoman . .*

The mill site looking north from the Mill Meadow to Admergill Barn. The track (right of picture) leads from the mill site to Blacko Bar.

Piles of cobblestones now litter the mill site as a yard has recently been taken up

We see, then, that John Hartley of Admergill took a share in Carr Mill in 1569. This suggests that there would not have been an operative mill at Admergill at the time of the above surrender as Hartley would have been unlikely to take a share in Carr Mill if he had a mill of his own. There is the possibility that he did indeed own Admergill as a working mill and was taking out shares in Carr Mill purely as a speculative venture – however, this would mean that he would have been competing against himself.

Finally, in a Recognizance Roll of 1634-35 we see that Benjamin Robertshaw, a corn miller of Blacko, admitted to *'bastardy on Anna Bannister.'* This, of course, does not mean that Robertshaw definitely ran a mill at Blacko, he could have been a miller at any place within the district. It is, nevertheless, an interesting record.

So, Admergill holds yet another secret. No doubt a serious archaeological survey of the Mill Meadow would go some way to uncovering the history buried there. It should be possible to locate the site of the building, along with datative evidence, and to find the siting of the weir, lodge and leats that would have played a vital role in the working of the mill.

Some interesting particulars of the obligation of customary tenants to grind at the Lord's Mill, and of the soke or multure to be taken by the Miller at the Lord's Mill, appear in a Custom Roll and Rental of the Manor of Assheton-under-Lyne dated 1422. *(Chetham Society,* Vol. LXXIV):

> *The tenants-at-will of the said lordship shall muller* [pay toll for grinding] *their corne growing upon the said tenements, at the Lord's milne to the sixteenth vessel, and they shall go to none other milne to muller their corn growing on their tenements, but to the Lord's milne; and which of them is found guilty of going to any other milne, they shall be highly amerced, and make fine at the Lord's will and if they buy corn, the which is dryed with the Lord's ffewel, they shall muller it at the Lord's milne to the sixteenth vessel, and all other corn that they buy they shall muller to the Lovesucken* [Old English Luf = favour; socn = privilege, i.e. the Miller's privilege to take toll for grinding. Lovesoken was a reduced charge for grinding corn that had been dried elsewhere], *which is to the twenty-fourth vessel, and go to none other milne if the com be bought within the said lordship.*
>
> *And the free tenants that oghen* [owe] *soken to the miln, shall muller as their chartours will, and as they have been accustomed of old time. And the free tenants and the tenants-at-will shall give the Milner his service* [or toll] *at all times, as it has been accustomed aforetime always; and if there be any default in the Milner's service that may be proved lawfully, he shall be punished highly by the Lord at his Courts, as the law and the custom will, and as has been used aforetime; and the customs of the milne shall be kept, every man to keep his grist, as has been sed aforetime; and when the Lord's corn come to the milne, he shall put all men out of their grist, and take their corn out of the hopper, if there be any therein, and his corn shall be ground next before all men, when it comes to the miln, without muller or paying service to the milner, but as of the kyng in capite his lyst and courtsy if he likes to give to the said miller.*

Chapter Eight

Final Thoughts

The *compotus* of the Abbott of Whalley (the abbey accounts) for the year 1422-23 show that the abbey estate rented '*the lands and a tenement called Blackhey*' and that Geoffrey Blakey held the land as undertenant to the abbey. In a late sixteenth century deposition regarding land holdings in Blacko a member of this Blakey family stated that following the 1507 deforestation of the area his grandfather had built the first house in Blacko. Was the tenement of 1422-23 a building at Admergill, perhaps on the site of the original monastic grange now occupied by Lower Admergill Hall?

In relation to the mound at **Site E** the Ightenhill estate records of 1395 show that two full-time *Moredrivars* were employed in the Pendle Forest for the *custodientes exire valebant* of the animals into the County of York. This meant that their task was to stop the forest deer from straying over the border between Admergill and Blacko into Barnoldswick and Middop, and also to prevent them being poached by outsiders. These moor drivers were provided with timber watch-towers from where they could monitor the movement of the animals and it is worth considering that the purpose of the mound at Admergill was to hold one of these towers.

Further to this we see within the Court Rolls that families by the name of Mankinholes were long term tenants of land at Blacko and neighbouring Roughlee. In 1392 a mower by the name of Richard Wilson Wilcockson received excessive payment of one shilling and three pence from Richard Mankinholes of Roughlee and Blacko. This was at a time when, as a consequence of the Black Death, the wages of agricultural workers had been strictly regulated and any person found to have been paid over the going rate was fined, along with his employer. Now, my point is that on the Blacko Hillside, above Malkin Tower Farm, is a field known as Mawkin Hole. Was this named after the gentry family of Mankinhole who tenanted the land? We know that Lower Admergill had been retained by the Crown in 1347 and this meant that it fell within Blacko. If a tower of sorts existed on the mound at Lower Admergill could that too have carried the name of the tenant, ie., Mankinhole Tower? You can see where this is going no doubt – Mankin was easily shortened to Malkin/Mawkin and so we would have site known as Malkin Tower. There is, then, at least the possibility that we have located the long-lost tower of local legend in which Old Demdike lived.

A William Mankinholes was a tenant in Blacko in 1443 and in 1564 James Folds, William Hanson and John Hartley of Admergill are recorded as renting land in Great Marsden from John Manknowles (this was the evolved spelling of Mankinholes), of Barker House in Great Marsden, thus providing a continuity of this family's tenure of Admergill within Blacko into the Tudor period. Folklore has it that the fabled Malkin Tower was destroyed after the witch trials of 1612 and we have a tentative date for the erection of Lower Admergill Hall of 1611 – give or take a year or so was the hall erected from the stonework incorporated into Malkin Tower? Food for thought if nothing else!

Much of the sitework within this paper is based upon the primary evidence of the Clitheroe estate records and evidence upon the ground. However, a main source of primary evidence has been the White Moor Map of 1580 and this is an excellent illustration of the value of sharing knowledge. If it had not been for Wilfred Spencer locating the map and bringing it home, and the generosity of Stanley Graham in making it available to the wider world, much of the information within the preceding text would not have come to light. Long may the spirit of sharing continue among local historians!

On the subject of the 1580 map it is fitting to relate part of the story of why it came into being. In the seventeenth year of the reign of Henry VII (1501) the overlord of Barnoldswick, one Henry Pudsey of Bolton Hall (Bolton-by-Bowland), wrote to the Chancellor of the Duchy of Lancaster stating that;

> *One Christopher Banaster in forcible manner contrarye to the order of lawe hathe wrongfully occupyed a parcell of me said farm called Brokden having thereunto no manner of title ... by the mynes whereof your orator is gretly endangereth and unabille to contente and pay his scale and is like to lose the land.*

This was a complaint against Christopher Bannister who lived in a house occupying the site of what is now the small chapel at the top of County Brook Lane (marked on the 1508 map as *Bannestre House*). Bannister had done little more than use the peat and water from the Black Brook which drained from the White Moor above his house, and taken advantage of what the tenants of Foulridge had always considered to be theirs by common right ie., White Moor up to Sandyford Head. Bannister duly answered Pudsey's complaint saying that;

> *The parcell of ground called Brollyn (Brogden) is the inheritance of our sovereign lord and the ferme thereunto is and hath been £7: 6s: 8d which by the space of thirty-eight years hath as well and truly at the days accustomed been paid.*
>
> Henry Pudsey then replies;
>
> *The plot defendant calls Browyn is also known as Brokden part of the fermehold of Henry which he allowed Xpher to occupy for three or four years unto such a tyme that Newarke field was where the Erle of Lincoln was slayne at which tyme the said Xpher being in the retynue of the said Henry then stole away from hym wherewith the said Henry was miscontented and warned hym thereupon to avoid the said ground.*
>
> The rejoinder of Christopher Banaster:
>
> *(He) Denies that he was with Henry at the said field or stole away as he hath of males surmysed. For he fond a man to do the kynge's grace service as the Retynue of the said Henry at the said tyme wherewith the said Henry was then contentyed.*

The nub of the matter was that there had been a long-simmering feud between the Bannisters of Foulridge and Henry Pudsey. This had its roots in the above accusation where Pudsey said that Christopher Bannister had forfeited any rights over common land he might have held of a knight's fee on White Moor because he had betrayed him, and his king, at the

Battle of Newark (Stoke) in 1487. Bannister was obligated to support his lord (Pudsey) at the battle but he elected instead to send a *proxy*, this was a man paid by Bannister to fulfil his duties in battle in his place. It would appear that Bannister's proxy duly turned up at Pudsey's side when the battle of Newark commenced but, as soon as he saw that the battle was hotting-up he duly legged it from the field!

Pudsey, quite rightly, took this less than chivalrous act to have been a failing on Bannister's part and pointed out that he should lose his rights to land held under a knight's fee. However, it is clear that Bannister carried on using the White Moor lands and water. The long-running feud between the two men might not have directly caused the land dispute between Foulridge and Barnoldswick but it certainly contributed and can be seen as an illustration of the complexity of land tenure within this area.

The Admergill valley taken from the Black Dyke

Looking over the Moorcock Inn and Greystones Moor through to Middop

Chapter Nine

Admergill Miscellany

One abiding problem with the records left to us by authorities, such as the Clitheroe estate, is that we rarely see the ordinary man and woman within them. These records were created so as to accurately record the business and land transactions of the upper echelons within society, or at least those wealthy enough to have rented land – thus we do not generally see the lives of the poor, the landless and the labourer. Gradually this was to change as the centuries passed. Poor Law records especially began to chart the existence of the person on the street and, by the time of the nineteenth century, the national census returns provide us with an invaluable insight into the lives of our forebears.

Following is an overview of the people of Admergill as they appear in records such as the Court Rolls, wills, land transactions and estate records. This is by no means a comprehensive list of those who have lived, worked and died within the shadow of the Blacko Hill, nor do we see the landless and the labourer, but we can put at least some flesh on the bones of the Admergill estate.

1524 Richard Tattersall sues John Hartley of Admergill for occupying several parcels of land in Barrowford. Jury says that the plaintiff shall have a way leading out of a close called Witley (Wheatley) for two years to come without interruption.

1537 James Hartley senior of Blacko sues James Hartley junior for trespass in obstructing a certain way in *'Le Bryghill up the Starbank'* (Bridge Hill on Star Bank was at Sandyford on the old Gisburn Road. This was a cross-roads where the track from Barnoldswick passed by Star Hall and down past the Moorcock Inn). The jury declared the defendant shall have a right of passage in each year from St. Martin until March for the carrying of dung (marl) and likewise between the feast of the Initiation of the Holy Cross until St. Michael the Archangel he shall drive his beasts to and fro to Bryghill and not at other times.

1537 James Hartley of Blacko fined 4d for keeping an objectionable dog *(canem irracionabilem)* to his neighbour's injury.

1539 Lawrence Robinson, Christopher Robinson, James Hartley (Admergill), John Smith (Admergill) and Henry Bannester versus Bernard Hartley, Henry Mitton (Ridge), Lawrence Hartley, Lawrence Hargreaves (Water Meetings), Christopher Blakey, John Hargreaves and James Hartley (Stone Edge) in a plea of trespass for obstructing a way leading from Wheathead Gate below Blacko Well to the Rayke (the corner of) upon Dry Clough and further to Stone Edge. Defendants guilty.

1539 Rentals: Over and Nether Barrowford

Christopher Robinson	£0	8s	3¾d
James Hartley jnr	£0	15s	3½d
John Smith	£0	7s	7¾d
Laurence Robinson	£0	7s	7¾d
John Robinson	£0	3s	9¾d
John Bucclyf	£0	3s	9¾d
James Hartley for Admergill	£0	7s	8¾d
James Hartley for part of Humphrey Hartley's land	£0	2s	0d
Laurence Wilson	£0	3s	10d
Christopher Blakey of Nether Barrowford	£0	5s	5½d
Laurence Hargreaves	£0	13s	11¾d
Bernard Hartley	£0	10s	11d
Laurence Hartley	£0	11s	1¾d
Margaret Hartley	£0	8s	2¾d
Margaret Hartley for part of Humphrey Hartley's land	£0	1s	0¾d
Henry Mitton	£0	8s	2¼
James Mitchell	£0	2s	1½d

1540 John Hartley and Bernard Hartley complain against Robert Blakey in a plea of trespass for open fences between Juddefield and the Long Rodes upon a dyke called *'Le Blacke Dyke.'* The jury awarded damages.

1549 Suite for ways between Lower Barrowford and Blacko - Bernard, Lawrence, James and Christopher Hartley, James Hartley of Fulshaw, James Hartley of Blacko, Lawrence and John Hargreaves, Lawrence Robinson, James Mitton and Lawrence Wilson versus Henry Bannester gent, Nicholas Smith and Christopher Robinson. Jury ordered a sufficient way to be kept between the Alms Kiln to a gap called Out Gait in Blacko (Blacko Gate in Admergill) on the land of Henry Bannester, Christopher Robinson and Nicholas Smith.

1551 A close of land at 9½ acres and 3s rent called Moor Hey at Blacko had been unlawfully occupied by Simon Blakey, son of Agnes and Nicholas Blakey of Admergill. Nicholas Blakey, son of Simon, took the said close with appurtenances at 3s.

1552 Land dispute - In 1551 Lawrence Hartley surrendered land in Barrowford at 4s to Christopher Hartley his son. James Hartley of Blacko disputed fine because of his inheritance. Dower reserved to Johanne late wife of Lawrence Hartley for life. In 1552 James Baldwin of Blacko seized the land at 10s. The jury ordered the land to return to Christopher Hartley.

1555 Nicholas, Lawrence and Bernard Hartley drove away their neighbour's beasts from pasture in Blacko.

1558 Richard Bancroft, Greave of Pendle Forest, surrenders a messuage (farm) in Fence at 10s to John Hartley of Admergill, Richard Hartley of Langroyde, Hugh Moor (son of Richard) and William Hargreaves of Higham.

1560 Inquisition elects John Hartley of Admergill as Greave of Colne.

1561 John Hartley of Admergill surrenders one parcel of land in and upon Blacko at 4s 8d to the use of Hugh Wilkinson, Jenett his wife and Elizabeth his daughter, and survivor, to the use of the following shall pay the Queen's rent and 14s to John Hartley, his heirs and assigns and 1 day of shearing, 1 day of turves drawing and 1 day of hay making.

1564 James Folds, William Hanson and John Hartley of Admergill surrender land in Great Marsden to John Manknowles and his heirs.

1608-09 Rentals: Over and Nether Barrowford

Laurence Townley of Carr esq		£1	5s	0d
Laurence Townley of Carr esq	Carr Mill	£1	0s	0d
Laurence Townley of Carr esq	Roughlee Mill	£0	2s	0d
Charles Bannester gent		£0	5s	8d
Simon Blakey gent		£0	3s	0d
John Hartley of Admergill		£1	19s	6d
Bernard Blakey		£0	2s	0d
Edward Robinson		£0	16s	0d
John Hargreaves		£1	10s	10½d
Lawrence Hartley		£1	9s	6d
Robert Hargreaves		£0	10s	8d
James Foulds		£0	5s	5d
Humphrey Hartley		£0	6s	4d
John Sutcliffe		£0	6s	8d
John & Nicholas Smith		£0	10s	9d
James Robinson		£0	16s	1½d
James Hartley		£0	10s	1¾d
Henry Shaw		£0	0s	7¾d
Robert Shaw		£0	6s	6½d
James Bulcock		£0	5s	5d
Christopher Blakey of Blacko		£0	10s	6d
Simon & Christopher Blakey		£0	3s	1d
John Parker		£0	1s	8d
Edward Marsden		£0	4s	8d
John Halsey & others for Wilson's land		£0	2s	6½d
Richard Hanson		£0	0s	2d

1622 John Hartley of Admergill surrenders 1 rood and ½ acre of land in Alkincoates to his son James Hartley.

1635 James Slater of Greystones, yeoman.

1662 William Hartley of Admergill has daughter Elizabeth.

1662 William Hartley of Admergill pays rent to the Duke of Albermarle of 6s 6d in 1618.

Admergill: Colne Parish Church Baptism Records

Elizabeth dtr of John Nutter de Admergill. John was the son of Alice Nutter of Roughlee (witch trials of 1612)	1600
Anna dtr of Jacobi Hartley de Admergill	1602
Bernard Hartley son of Jacobi Hartley de Admergill	1600
Margreta Hartley dtr of Jacobi Hartley de Admergill	1606
Johes Hartley son of Jacobi Hartley de Admergill	1608
Jacobus Hartley son of Jacobi Hartley de Admergill	1610
Robt Hartley son of Jacobi Hartley de Admergill	1613
Hugo Hartley son of Jacobi Hartley de Admergill	1619
Johanis son of Gulielmi (William) Hartley	1640
Gulielmus son of Gulielmi Hartley	1645
Anna dtr of Gulielmi Hartley	1647
Jane dtr of Gulielmi Hartley	1642
Jacob son of Gulielmi Hartley	1649
Ellen dtr of Gulielmi Hartley	1654
George son of Gulielmi Hartley	1655
Ellen dtr of Gulielmi Hartley	1657
Margaret dtr of Gulielmi Hartley	1660
Elizabeth dtr of Gulielmi Hartley	1662
Jane dtr of Gulielmi Hartley	1667
Ann dtr of Gulielmi Hartley	1677
Ellin dtr of John Hartley of Roughlee and Admergill	1664
William son of John Hartley of Roughlee and Admergill	1667
Jane dtr of John Hartley of Roughlee and Admergill	1679
William son of James Hartley	1616
Margaretta illegit dtr of Crofern Baldwyne of Wheathead	1609
Crofern son of Johnes Baldwyne	1630
Xpofer son of Xpofri Baldwyne	1659
Nicholas son of Xpofri Baldwyne	1646
John son of John Stephenson	1648
Elizabeth dtr of William Hanson	1639

Admergill: Colne Parish Church Baptism Records (Continued)

Ellena dtr of William Hanson	1621
Jenetta dtr of William Hanson	1624
Grace dtr of William Hanson	1631
Isabella dtr of William Hanson	1637
Robert son of Richardi Nowell	1621
Priscilla dtr of Johnes Blakey	1612
Isabella dtr of Johnes Blakey	1614
Henric son of James Whitaker	1602
John son of James Whitaker	1611
Elizabeth dtr of James Whitaker	1613
Johanes illegit son of Christopher Emotson	1641
Maria Hanson dtr of John Hanson and Maria Hargreaves	1677
William son of John Stevenson	1660
Richard son of John Stevenson	1663
Barbara dtr of John Stevenson	1666
Ann Sellar dtr of William Stephenson	1693

1663 John Hartley of Admergill married Ellen Hartley of Roughlee Hall. Ellen was the daughter of James Hartley of Roughlee Hall who inherited the Dimpenley estate and moved there. James was the son of Margaret Smith, of Roughlee Hall and Hugh Hartley, yeoman of Winewall. Margaret's father, John Smith is thought to have built Roughlee Hall, he married Alice Shaw, daughter of Henry Shaw of Newsome, later of Blacko. Alice later married a Slater.

Colne Wills: Admergill:

John Hartley	1623	
Margaret Hartley	1632	
James Hartley	1801	Worsted manufacturer.

Whittaker states in his *'History of Whalley'* that:

> *Admergill . . . Here were lately* (written 1801) *found 117 pennies of Edward 1st and John Baliol, King of Scotland.*

1567 Copy of court roll of admittance of Robert Rushworth, Alexander Hartley, son of John Hartley of Admergill, and John Whittacre, son of Laurence Whitacre to 27 acres in High Whittacre, as a result of an indenture of 3rd April 1567. Reciting a surrender of 24th November 1566.

1567 John Hartley of Admergill in Barrowford Booth, along with Nicholas Starkie, son of Edmund Starkie, gent., Robert Rushworth, Alexander Hartley and John Whittaker, is recipient of a messuage called High Whittacre with land in High Whittacre, Padiham, Whalley, Clitheroe and Simonstone.

1589 Alexander Hartley, son of John Hartley of Admergill, Yorks., gent., surrenders 27 acres of land to John Whitaker as part of High Whitaker, Padiham.

1598 Surrender in the Halmot Court of Colne: Barnard Parker of Alkincoots and Richard Kepas of Marseden, trustees for James son and heir of John Mitchell of Colne, deceased, to Alexander Hartley of Admergill: for £53: -- 2 messuages, 2 barns and a garden, in the tenure of Richard Fenton, John Blakay and the widow of John Mitchell -- fine 8d.

1613 John Hartley of Admergill, co. York, yeoman, to Alexander Hartley of Langrod, clothier: a bond for £60 from Francis Carr of Blacow and Emery Carr of Colne, gents.

1631 Inquisition: fine 14d: on the oaths of John Stephenson of Goldshawe, John Moore of Greenhead, John Hargreves of Barowford, junior, Miles Nutter of Roughlie (son of Alice Nutter), Christofer Robinson of Barcley, John Higgin of the same, Christoffer Vareley of Whitleybooth, Richard Hartley of the same, William Stevenson of Stainscome, Richard Moore of Fence, Lawrence Stevenson of the same, Lawrence Robinson of Goldshaw, John Nutter of the same, Barnard Sutcliffe of Pasture and James Robinson of Barowford, who say that John Hartley of Admergill, trustee of Nicholas Mitchell of Colne, William Sagar of Catlowe and John Hargreves of Greenfeild, died seized of one-fifth part of lands in Overbarowford below the Stonebrig lately built in the Overbarowford (the 'Roman Bridge') now in the tenure of John Robinson of Goldshay and that Elizabeth wife of John Robinson of Oldlaund and Ellen, daughter and co-heir of Alexander Hartley, son of John Hartley, are the next heirs of JohnHartley.

1622 Admittance of the court of the manor of Colne of James son of John Hartley of Admergill to -- 1 rood and ½ acre of land in Alkincotes and Colne -- surrendered by John Hartley.

1632 Surrender: John Robinson of Oldlawnd, Elizabeth his wife and Ellen Hartley late of Admergill: Elizabeth and Ellen being heirs of John Hartley of Admergill, deceased, at the request of John Robinson of Goldshay son and heir of Margaret his mother to the use of John Robinson

1669 Civil action (cause unknown): Henery Banaster of Parkehill versus Richard Towneley of Carre, esq., William Hartley of Admergill, John Hargreaves of Higham, Andrew Holden, and John Whaley.

1691 Will of Christopher Hanson of Roughleigh in the Forest of Pendle: -- a messuage in Roughlee and Roughlee Booth to Henry Ryecroft of Fullshaw and Henry Robinson of Carr Hall, in trust to the use of daughter Alison, *'who liveth with me,'* for one year after his death, then to the use of son William, of Thornyholme, husbandman, subject to 20s yearly to Alison who was to have occupation of *'the parlor in the house in which I now live'* for life; 20s each to grand-daughters Isabell and Ellen, daughters of John Hanson of Admergill, County York, deceased, out of personal estate after payment of debts and funeral expenses.

1708 Alexander Hartley of Barraford, yeoman, to George Hartley of Barnoldswick, mercer, and James Bulcock of Barraford, yeoman -- messuage at Admirgill, with 3 barns, 1 garden, 2 orchards, & closes called Bean Croft, Croft, Meadow on backside of House, Benty Sett, Birk Dole, Sheep Coat Meadow, Long Hey, Football Ing, Olding Dole, Money Gates, New Field, Barly Holme Banke, Over Field, Dole, Dole Holme, & Admirgill Pasture (100 acres) – Witnessed by Christopher Taylor, James Stansfield and John Oxnard.

1725 Will of William Kaley of Hobstone, gent -- to George Halstead of Lower Bradley and James Smith of Langrod, yeomen, messuages called Ball Brigg and Hobstones, in trust for daughter Betty and grandaughter Betty Kaley. Property in Higher Admergill and Sawley, County York, to his daughter for life then to his granddaughter.

1725 John Stephenson is at Admergill and owned a tenement adjoining Hobstones.

1757 Release: for £600: John Hartley of Whitelee, mercer, to Jacob Costabadie of York, gent. -- messuage & closes in Admergill in the tenure of Paul Greenwood, Peter Hall and John Hall – Witnessed by William Wailes and Thomas Preston junior.

1816 John Hartley of Admergill, in the liberty of Admergill & Brogden, farmer, buys a plot of land 344 square yards, part of The Doles belonging to Watermeetings Farm.

1841 John William Speak was born at Admergill in 1870 his parents, Charles and Mary Speak, farmed there and prior to that Charles parents John and Elizabeth Speak were there in the 1841 census. John, William's brother Brown Speak, farmed at Higher Wheathead for many years and their brother, Jonathan Brown, also farmed at Admergill.

1863 Exemplification of Recovery: Alexander Hartley, plaintiff, and John Hartley and Jane his wife, deforciants -- 1 messuage, 3 barns, 1 garden, 2 orchards, 4 acres of land, 4 acres of land, 4 acres of meadow and 100 acres of pasture in Admergill.

1873 Land Tax
Executors of S. Garnett of Admergill pay £36.10s rental for 39 acres – 2 roods – 21 perches

Men aged 18 to 50 in the year 1760

BROGDEN and ADMERGILL

John Smith.......New House
Rich'd Edmondson......New House
Tho. Edmondson......Lidget Flat
Joseph Wigglesworth
Andrew Slater
Thomas Dean snr
William Hartley..........Brogden
Ralph Slater
John Slater
Richard Shutt
John Harrison

Thomas Dean jnr
Henry Dean jnr
Henry Dean snr
John Greenwood........Coverdale
John Armistead..........Coverdale
Johnathan Moor
James Hartley.......Admergill
George Hartley snr
John Hartley..........Admergill
George Hartley jnr
James Manley
Moses Wilkinson
Hammond Baldwin
John Ormerod
Peter Hall
Thomas Hall
John Hargreaves
William Folds
Robert Folds
Roger Broughton......Bar

Note:
This list is part of the Oakes Deeds which are kept at Sheffield City Archives and bears ref. OD1178/18. Courtesy of K. Ranson.

It is quite clear from the above snippets that the Hartley family have been the virtual lords of Admergill for centuries. The following is a resume on the family:

THE HARTLEYS OF ADMERGILL AND WHITELEE IN PENDLE FOREST

From the Calendar of Lancashire Documents: (courtesy of Stanley Graham)

James Hartley of Admergill in the county of York by his will dated 1642 left that estate to his son William Hartley, who's son and heir, John Hartley of Admergill appears to have died in 1699m having had issue. Alexander, William, John, James, George, Anne and Margaret. The eldest son Alexander succeeded his father and had a son, John Hartley, who sold the Admergill estate to his uncle John Hartley in 1726.

William Hartley (second son of John, who died in 1699) married Ellen Robinson of Roughlee and was ancestor of the late William Hartley, gent, of Fence Gate in the Forest of Pendle. He married Elizabeth, daughter of Mr Nicholas Grimshaw of Higham, and he had with a son William Hartley baptised at New Church in Pendle 18th June 1797, died unmarried. The following daughters: Mary baptised 17th February 1788 died unmarried. Susannah baptised 23rd May 1790 married Mr John Robertshaw and is now resident at Fence Gate. Margaret baptised 2nd September 1792 died unmarried. Ann, baptised 8th December 1799died unmarried. Agnes, baptised 24th of April 1803 died unmarried and Ellen baptised 30th of March 1806 died unmarried.

Margaret Hartley (Third daughter of William Hartley by his wife Elizabeth Grimshaw) married Mr Henry Waddington and had issue an only son and heir, Henry Waddington Hartley Esq of Fence Gate who married Susan, daughter of Harry Bolton Esq. Of Colne, solicitor by his wife Elizabeth Ann, daughter of Henry Hargreaves Esq., of Newchurch in Rossendale. And has issue a son and daughter.

John Hartley of Newchurch in Pendle and Higher White Lee in Pendle Forest (an estate which was acquired by purchase about the close of the 17th or the beginning of the last century) was the third son of John Hartley of Admergill who died in 1699. He had issue two sons, John and George and four daughters, Jane married to Mr John Manknowles, Elizabeth married to the Revd. Mr Nabbs of Newchurch in Pendle, Mrs Cronkshaw and Mary Married to Mr Bernard Hartley of the Hague near Colne.

John Hartley, Gent., of Higher White Lee (elder son of the above John Hartley) was party to a surrender dated 17th April 1765 , the other parties being Christopher Shackleton of Stone Edge in the Forest of Pendle and Bernard Hartley of White Lee, son of the said John Hartley. Mr John Hartley died in 1770 (buried at Newchurch in Pendle 7th of March 1770having had by Elizabeth his wife, (buried at Newchurch Aug 2nd 1768) the following children: John, Bernard, James (buried 1st Feb 1759) George died unmarried, Elizabeth died unmarried, Alice, baptised 10th November 1741 married Mr Southeron of York. Catherine, baptised 8th February 1745/46 died unmarried. Mary, baptised 1st August 1747/8 buried 16th October 1748. Jane baptised 11th April 1754buried 2nd July 1759. Ellen buried 23 January 1768.

John Hartley, of Blackburn, surgeon, Late of Whitelee was eldest son of John by Elizabeth his wife. He married Ann Brooks (buried 27th December 1761) and had an only son and heir.

Revd. John Hartley D.LL. Brazenose College, Oxford, incumbent of Colne baptised at Blackburn 30th of January 1760. he was JP for the county and died unmarried at Colne May 1811 aged 51. His brother Bernard Hartley, gent of Lower Whitelee, (2nd son of John Hartley) built the present house of Lower White Lee and married Sarah, daughter of Mr William Roberts of Ightenhill by whom he had issue; John, died unmarried; James, buried April 9th 1775; William, buried 23rd December 1781; Bernard, Alexander, Jane died unmarried; Sarah married Mr James Topper of Burnley, Elizabeth married Mr John Kenyon of Accrington, Mary married Mr John Heeles of Whitebank near Bolton and Ann buried 13th March 1793.

Bernard Hartley died in May 1797 buried 18th May. His son was Bernard Hartley of Lower White Lee. He married Ellen Haworth and died in 1750, buried on 26th April aged 68 leaving an only son.

Bernard Hartley of Lower White Lee gent., was twice married. First to Miss Margaret Ann Topper, by whom he had a daughter who died young. Second to Ann, daughter of Mr John Grimshaw of Bank House in Higham. He died in 1858 aged 25 years buried at Fence April 23rd leaving no issue.

Alexander Hartley, younger surviving son of Bernard Hartley who died in 1797, married Maria Crook and had issue a son, Mr John Hartley, printer, Colne who now possesses the estates of Lower White Lee and Admergill; and three daughters, Alice, wife of Mr Law, surgeon of Padiham. Sarah, wife of Mr Henry Johnson of Rochdale, and Jane, wife of Mr Doyle of Colne, surgeon. Mr Alexander Hartley died June 1839 and was buried June 20th aged 56 years.

The Turnpike Road

In 1842 Admergill played a small part within the history of our road system. At the Nisi Prius Court of the Yorkshire Spring Assizes, a case was heard that was to settle the thorny question as to who was responsible for the upkeep of the public roads within the parishes of England. The inhabitants of Admergill were prosecuting and were represented by Mr. Baines, Mr. Hall and Mr. Ashmore. Opposing them were Mr. Dundas, Mr. Stansfield and Sir Gregory Allnutt Lewin. This latter was a Yorkshire barrister well known for representing the underdog. The son of Richard Lewin, of Kent, Sir Gregory been elected to the Infant School Society in 1824 and the Society of Antiquarians in 1833 and in the following year he represented the five accused in the famous Cockermouth Murder Trial. The accused were indicted on a charge of murdering a young collier from Cockermouth but in a single hearing, lasting over ten hours, Lewin won the day and his clients walked free. In 1840 he represented a number of men who had taken part in an uprising of Sheffield Chartists but he was not successful at this particular trial. By 1845 (the year of his death) Lewin had become the recorder for Doncaster and had written eight books and reports on English law. It is clear that Mr. Baines, the attorney acting for Admergill, had his work cut out in opposing Lewin.

The crux of the case against Admergill was that a government inquiry had found that of the five townships within the parish of Barnoldswick ie., Coates, Barnoldswick, Brogden, Admergill and Salterforth, only Admergill had elected not to employ its own surveyor with a view to maintaining the public road running through the township. The turnpike road (to become the A682) had been built in 1804 it was generally accepted that each township should repair its own portion of the highway, otherwise the whole parish would be responsible for the townships who neglected their duties. The question arose as to whether Admergill could be said to have been a township as it was considered to have been Brogden-cum-Admergill and, although Brogden and Admergill had been united in their obligations to the poor, they were separate for highway and church rates. However, the judge agreed that for the purposes of the hearing it would be called a township.

The prosecution stated that until the past two years Admergill had no attorney although one had gone to live there recently and had *'furbished up some musty old records to persuade the farmers it was better for them to continue repairing the road in the same comfortable way that their fathers had done before them.'* A number of witnesses were called in defence of the Admergill farmers and plans of the parish and roadways were offered to the judge. Having perused them with a jaundiced eye the judge observed that; *'It is strange that surveyors would not learn to make plans that could be made useful. These plans are so unwieldy that they cannot be handled; and then they could not be understood!'*

On some evidence it was clear that distant surveyors had been employed and some outlying townships of Barnoldswick had repaired their own roads. Baines stated that there was no proof of there having been a public highway through Admergill before 1804 although the surveyor who had drawn the plan before the court thought that he had found traces of an ancient road. The history of the case was that prior to 1804 the public road from Colne to Gisburn had gone through Barnoldswick and Brogden and not an inch of it had been in Admergill. Baines went on to say that in 1804 the present road had been made, with 1½ miles of it being in Admergill, and if the verdict went against him the effect would be to burden the poor inhabitants of Admergill, who had before nothing to do with this road, with the repairs for all time. There was no proof of any public highway before 1804 as there had been only occupation roads from Gisburn Old Road down to the individual farmsteads.

It was true that when the new road needed repairing the farmers grouped together, perhaps being threatened by the lawyer (Stansfield) who urged his learned friend (Lewin) on. The farmers had agreed to parcel the road out among themselves *'for quietness sake, and to prevent having the lawyers on their backs,'* as one witness said. A consequence of this was that now the opposition were attempting to saddle these seven poor fellows with the expense of maintaining the said road forever.

Lewin summed up by saying that a previous, similar case showed the other four townships within Barnoldswick had appointed district surveyors and repaired their own road and so this should be the case with the one remaining township of Admergill. There should be agreement between all townships that each repair their own road independently of the parish. The verdict of the court was for the defendants and so it was established that it was the custom for each township to repair their own roads.

The 1853 OS map of Admergill shows only four farms within the estate but there are stated to have been seven within Admergill in 1842. The seven farms are taken to have been Burn Moor End, Higher Admergill, Lower Admergill, One Tree Hill, Admergill Pasture, Moorcock and Greystones. The Moorcock was a farming inn at the time and One Tree Hill became known as Blacko Tower Farm and, in the later nineteenth century, Jonathan Stansfield bought this latter property. Stansfield was a well-know business man from Barrowford and, in 1890, built the tower upon his land of Blacko Hill. This landmark was known originally as Jonathan's Tower and Stansfield's Folly before the name finally settled as Blacko Tower. It is interesting to note that One Tree Hill Farm was probably named after Blacko Hill beneath which it sat, thus suggesting that Blacko Hill was formerly known as One Tree Hill. There is a local legend that persists to this day that a tunnel connects Blacko Hill with Lower Admergill and we probably have here a folk memory of a connection (a dyke or a ditch?) between the two within the mists of time.

It would be fascinating to know what shape the Blacko Hill took before half of its bulk was quarried away. There can be little doubt that such a prominent landmark (at 1,000 feet) would have been of great importance to our forebears, especially within pre-history. In the 1950s a nice example of a bronze axe-head was found on the top of the hill and this begs the question as to how many other ancient artefacts were lost from here during two centuries of quarrying operations?

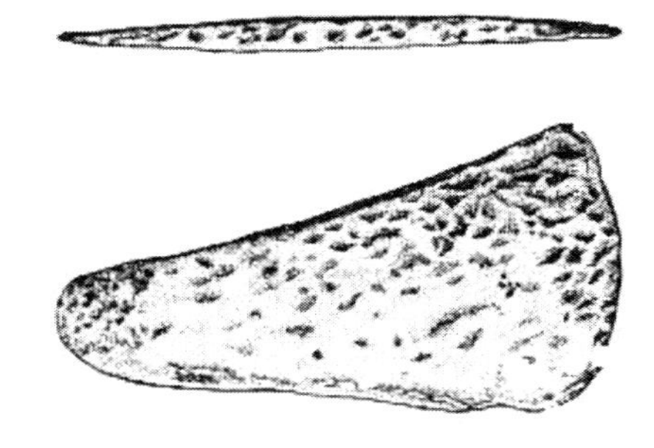

The axe-head found on Blacko Hill in 1957

Finally

We have looked around Admergill with a weather-eye cocked to the possibilities of early settlement within the estate. The huge boulders lying almost buried on the slopes of Green bank offer tantalising clues to the existence of pre-historic occupation hereabouts. This is furthered by the discovery of the bowl quern, an artefact that has perhaps lain unused within Admergill for almost three millennia.

Within the defended mound are clues to a troubled and turbulent past belied by the present quiet solitude of the Admergill valley. Without archaeological evidence it is perhaps best to leave the mystery of this mound as just that – until we know better it is fair to say that the site offers itself up as secret testimony to the development of today's world.

There is every possibility that we have seen where the inhabitants of Admergill lived and worked for centuries within the Medieval, and later Tudor periods. The site of the Admergill Houses awaits further research and surely this would provide an insight into the lives of the ordinary people who built their hamlet in this now-remote place, laboured on the land and raised their families there.

Lower Admergill Hall stands as testimony to the wealth of the woollen industry. It is probable that either the Blakey family or the Hartley family built the Hall in the earlier part of the seventeenth century when they would have been keen to broadcast their status to the world through the medium of stone, in place of timber. We have seen that the Blakey family are recorded as having erected the first house in Blacko in the earlier part of the sixteenth century; they were certainly at Admergill at that time - and we also see in the Colne baptisms that a John Blakey was baptising his children at Admergill in 1612 and 1614. Both the Blakey and Hartley families were woollen dealers and had acquired enough wealth by the sixteenth century to erect the type of building we see in the Hall.

The 'Monastery,' as the earlier building here was known, would have been built for the same purpose, and by the same people, at an earlier date than the extant Hall. However, it is difficult to see that the appellation of 'Monastery' fits in with the known history of the site in as much as the Kirkstall and Fountains Abbeys had lost their tenure of Admergill in the fourteenth century. Having said that, there is the possibility that other ecclesiastical tenants, in the form of Whalley Abbey, held the 'Monastery' as a grange until the 1530-40s when the Dissolution put an end to their land holdings.

The exact site of the Admergill Mill is, as yet, undiscovered but even a cursory archaeological survey would probably reveal its whereabouts. What is more difficult to ascertain is the date at which the mill operated and who actually owned it. Perhaps it would be best, for the time being, to leave the mill with the suggestion that it would have been built, and operated, by either the Kirkstall monks, the Whalley monks, the Blakeys or the Hartleys. Until such times that we know for sure this might prove to be reasonably close to the truth.

* * * * *

That, for the time being, concludes this tour of the Admergill estate. I hope that I have managed to convey the sense of hidden history that this valley holds within its bracken-strewed banks. Miraculously the valley has escaped the ravages of our modern thirst for development, despite the fact that the arterial route of the A682 cuts unceremoniously across its eastern flank. It is difficult to think of another self-contained area such as Admergill where there is such strong evidence for continual inhabitation stretching, perhaps, over millennia. It would be satisfying to see at least some of the projected sites within the above text giving up some of their secrets but this is not likely without the attention of a professional body. In the meantime the Admergill valley sits quietly on our doorstep, unassuming and undemanding – awaiting the next nosey-parker to come along and furtle among its stones and ditches!

This stone clapper bridge takes a footpath across Admergill Water and up to the Moorcock Inn.

This is one of three such bridges still remaining in situ within the Admergill valley

I am grateful to Stanley Graham BA for photographs and information used within this book.

Thanks are also extended to Simon Dalgleish, owner of Lower Admergill, for his generosity in allowing us to wander his land with camera and spade.

Also to Maurice Horsefield, of Higher Sandyford Farm, for information relating to the land of White Moor.

Bibliography

Bennet, W. *The History of Burnley* – Vols 1 & 2. (1946) Burnley District Council.
Blakey, J. *The Annals and Stories of Barrowford.* (1929). SP.
Brigg, M. *The Early History of the Forest of Pendle.* Pendle Heritage.
Brown, P. *Megaliths, Myths and Men.* (1976) Book Club Associates.
Carr, J. *Annals and Stories of Colne.* (1878)
Clayton, J. A. *The Valley of the Drawn Sword. History of Burnley, Pendle and West Craven.* (2006). Barrowford Press.
Clayton, J. A. *The Lancashire Witch Conspiracy. A History of Pendle Forest and the 1612 Witch Trials.* (2007). Barrowford Press.
Crowther, D. Misc. unpublished papers held at Nelson Local Studies Libraries.
Farrar, W. *Clitheroe Court Rolls.* (1912) Vols 1, 2 & 3.
Gardner, W. *Ancient Earthworks – Lancashire South of the Sands.*
Gelling, M. and Cole, A. *The Landscape of Place-names.* (2000). Stamford
Harrison, D. *The History of Colne.* (1998). Pendle Heritage.
Hodgkiss and Bagley. *A History of the County Palatine of Lancaster in Early Maps.* (1985)
Kenyon, D. *The Origins of Lancashire.* (1991). Manchester University Press.
Lancashire Archaeological Unit. *The Archaeology of Lancashire* (1996)
Pearson, S. *Rural Houses of the Lancashire Pennines.* (1985). English Heritage.
Smith, R. *Blackburnshire* (occ. paper). University of Leicester.
Warner, J. H. *The History of Barnoldswick.* (1934)
Welch, M. *Anglo-Saxon England.* (1992). English Heritage.
Whitaker, T. D. *The History of Whalley.* (1st ed. 1801).
Whitaker, T. D. *The History of the Deanery of Craven. (3rd ed.)*
Whittaker, G. *Roughlee Hall – Fact and Fiction.* (1980). Nelson Hist. Soc.

© John A Clayton